DEVELOPMENT

IN PRACTICE

Curbing the Epidemic
Governments and the
Economics of Tobacco Control

D1531163

Curbing the Epidemic
Governments and the
Economics of Tobacco Control

THE WORLD BANK
WASHINGTON D.C.

HV
5732
.J43
1999

The findings, interpretations, and conclusions expressed in this paper are entirely those of the author(s) and should not be attributed in any manner to the World Bank, to its affiliated organizations, or to members of its Board of Executive Directors or the countries they represent. The World Bank does not guarantee the accuracy of the data included in this publication and accepts no responsibility for any consequence of their use.

The material in this publication is copyrighted. The World Bank encourages dissemination of its work and will normally grant permission to reproduce portions of the work promptly.

Permission to *photocopy* items for internal or personal use, for the internal or personal use of specific clients, or for educational classroom use is granted by the World Bank, provided that the appropriate fee is paid directly to the Copyright Clearance Center, Inc., 222 Rosewood Drive, Danvers, MA 01923, USA.; telephone 978-750-8400, fax 978-750-4470. Please contact the Copyright Clearance Center before photocopying items.

For permission to *reprint* individual articles or chapters, please fax a request with complete information to the Republication Department, Copyright Clearance Center, fax 978-750-4470.

All other queries on rights and licenses should be addressed to the Office of the Publisher, World Bank, at the address above or faxed to 202-522-2422.

Cover photo: Dr. Joe Losos, Health Canada

ISBN 0-8213-4519-2

Library of Congress Cataloging-in-Publication Data

Jha, Prabhat, 1965–
    Curbing the epidemic : governments and the economics of
tobacco control / Prabhat Jha, Frank J. Chaloupka
        p.   cm. — (Development in practice)
    Includes bibliographical references.
    ISBN 0-8213-4519-2
        1. Tobacco habit—Government policy.   2. Tobacco habit—Government
    policy—Cost effectiveness.   I. Chaloupka, Frank J.   II. Title.
    III. Series: Development in practice (Washington, D.C.)
    HV5732.J43   1999
    363.4—dc21   99-29266
                                                                              CIP

Contents

FIGURES

Foreword

WITH current smoking patterns, about 500 million people alive today will eventually be killed by tobacco use. More than half of these are now children and teenagers. By 2030, tobacco is expected to be the single biggest cause of death worldwide, accounting for about 10 million deaths per year. Increased activity to reduce this burden is a priority for both the World Health Organization (WHO) and the World Bank as part of their missions to improve health and reduce poverty. By enabling efforts to identify and implement effective tobacco control policies, particularly in children, both organizations would be fulfilling their missions and helping to reduce the suffering and costs of the smoking epidemic.

Tobacco is different from many other health challenges. Cigarettes are demanded by consumers and form part of the social custom of many societies. Cigarettes are extensively traded and profitable commodities, whose production and consumption have an impact on the social and economic resources of developed and developing countries alike. The economic aspects of tobacco use are therefore critical to the debate on its control. However, until recently these aspects have received little global attention.

This report aims to help fill that gap. It covers key issues that most societies and policymakers face when they think about tobacco or its control. The report is an important part of the partnership between the WHO and the World Bank. The WHO, the principal international agency on health issues, has taken the lead in responding to the epidemic with its Tobacco Free Initiative. The World Bank aims to work in partnership with the lead agency, offering its particular analytic resources in economics. Since 1991, the World Bank has had a formal policy on tobacco, in recognition of the harm that it does to health. The policy prohibits the Bank from lending on tobacco and encourages control efforts.

The report is also timely. In light of the rising death toll from tobacco, many governments, nongovernmental organizations, and agencies within the United Nations (UN) system, such as UNICEF and the Food and Agricultural Organization, and the International Monetary Fund are examining their own policies on tobacco control. This report draws on many productive collaborations that have arisen from such reviews at national and international levels.

This report is intended mainly to address the concerns raised by policymakers about the impact of tobacco control policies on economies. The benefits of tobacco control for health, especially for the world's children, are clear. There are, however, costs to tobacco control, and policymakers need to weigh these carefully. In cases where tobacco control policies impose costs on the poorest in society, governments clearly have a responsibility to help reduce these costs through, for example, transition schemes for poor tobacco farmers.

Tobacco is among the greatest causes of preventable and premature deaths in human history. Yet comparatively simple and cost-effective policies that can reduce its devastating impact are already available. For governments intent on improving health within the framework of sound economic policies, action to control tobacco represents an unusually attractive choice.

David de Ferranti
Vice President
Human Development Network
The World Bank

Jie Chen
Executive Director
Noncommunicable Diseases
World Health Organization

Report team: This report was prepared by a team led by Prabhat Jha, and included Frank J. Chaloupka (co-lead), Phyllida Brown, Son Nguyen, Jocelyn Severino-Marquez, Rowena van der Merwe, and Ayda Yurekli. William Jack, Nicole Klingen, Maureen Law, Philip Musgrove, Thomas E. Novotny, Mead Over, Kent Ranson, Michael Walton, and Abdo Yazbeck provided valuable input and advice. This report benefited from substantive early work on tobacco at the World Bank by Howard Barnum. Input from the World Health Organization was provided by Derek Yach, and input from the U.S. Centers for Disease Control and Prevention was provided by Michael Eriksen. The work was carried out under the general direction of Helen Saxenian, Christopher Lovelace, and David de Ferranti. Richard Feachem was instrumental in initiating this report. Any errors are the report team's own.

The production staff of the report included Dan Kagan, Don Reisman, and Brenda Mejia.

The report benefited greatly from a wide variety of consultations (see Acknowledgments in Appendix C). Support for this report came from the Human Development Network of the World Bank, the Institute for Social and Preventive Medicine, University of Lausanne, and the Office on Smoking and Health at the U.S. Centers for Disease Control and Prevention. Their assistance is warmly acknowledged.

Preface

THIS report has its origins in the converging efforts of several partners to address a shared problem: the relative neglect of economic contributions to the debate on tobacco control. In 1997, at the 10th World Conference on Tobacco in Beijing, China, the World Bank organized a consultation session on the economics of tobacco control. The meeting was part of an ongoing review of the Bank's own policies. There was clear recognition at this meeting that insufficient global attention was being paid to the economics of the smoking epidemic. The meeting's participants also agreed that the discipline of economics was not being applied to tobacco control in many countries, and that even where economic approaches were being used, their methodology was of variable quality.

At the same time that the World Bank began reviewing its policies, economists at the University of Cape Town, South Africa, had begun a project on the economics of tobacco control for Southern Africa. These initiatives were brought together, in partnership with economists at the University of Lausanne, Switzerland, and others, to form a wider review. The work culminated in a conference in Cape Town in February 1998. The proceedings of that conference are published separately.[1] The collaboration led to a broader analysis of the economics of tobacco control, involving economists and others from a wide range of countries and institutions. Some of the studies resulting from this analysis will be published shortly.[2] This report summarizes the findings of those studies that are relevant to policymakers.

Notes

1. Abedian, Iraj, R. van der Merwe, N. Wilkins, and P. Jha. eds. 1998. *The Economics of Tobacco Control: Towards an Optimal Policy Mix*. University of Cape Town, South Africa.

2. *Tobacco Control Policies in Developing Countries*. Jha, Prabhat and F. Chaloupka, eds. Oxford University Press, forthcoming.

Summary

SMOKING already kills one in 10 adults worldwide. By 2030, perhaps a little sooner, the proportion will be one in six, or 10 million deaths per year—more than any other single cause. Whereas until recently this epidemic of chronic disease and premature death mainly affected the rich countries, it is now rapidly shifting to the developing world. By 2020, seven of every 10 people killed by smoking will be in low- and middle-income nations.

Why this report?

Few people now dispute that smoking is damaging human health on a global scale. However, many governments have avoided taking action to control smoking—such as higher taxes, comprehensive bans on advertising and promotion, or restrictions on smoking in public places—because of concerns that their interventions might have harmful economic consequences. For example, some policymakers fear that reduced sales of cigarettes would mean the permanent loss of thousands of jobs; that higher tobacco taxes would result in lower government revenues; and that higher prices would encourage massive levels of cigarette smuggling.

This report examines the economic questions that policymakers must address when contemplating tobacco control. It asks whether smokers know the risks and bear the costs of their consumption choices, and explores the options for governments if they decide that intervention is justified. The report assesses the expected consequences of tobacco control for health, for econo-

1

mies, and for individuals. It demonstrates that the economic fears that have deterred policymakers from taking action are largely unfounded. Policies that reduce the demand for tobacco, such as a decision to increase tobacco taxes, would not cause long-term job losses in the vast majority of countries. Nor would higher tobacco taxes reduce tax revenues; rather, revenues would climb in the medium term. Such policies could, in sum, bring unprecedented health benefits without harming economies.

Current trends

About 1.1 billion people smoke worldwide. By 2025, the number is expected to rise to more than 1.6 billion. In the high-income countries, smoking has been in overall decline for decades, although it continues to rise in some groups. In low- and middle-income countries, by contrast, cigarette consumption has been increasing. Freer trade in cigarettes has contributed to rising consumption in these countries in recent years.

Most smokers start young. In the high-income countries, about eight out of 10 begin in their teens. While most smokers in low- and middle-income countries start in the early twenties, the peak age of uptake in these countries is falling. In most countries today, the poor are more likely to smoke than the rich.

The health consequences

The health consequences of smoking are twofold. First, the smoker rapidly becomes addicted to nicotine. The addictive properties of nicotine are well documented but are often underestimated by the consumer. In the United States, studies among final-year high school students suggest that fewer than two out of five smokers who believe that they will quit within five years actually do quit. About seven out of 10 adult smokers in high-income countries say they regret starting, and would like to stop. Over decades and as knowledge has increased, the high-income countries have accumulated a substantial number of former smokers who have successfully quit. However, individual attempts to quit have low success rates: of those who try without the assistance of cessation programs, about 98 percent will have started again within a year. In low- and middle-income countries, quitting is rare.

Smoking causes fatal and disabling disease, and, compared with other risky behaviors, the risk of premature death is extremely high. Half of all long-term smokers will eventually be killed by tobacco, and of these, half will die during productive middle age, losing 20 to 25 years of life. The diseases associated with smoking are well documented and include cancers of the lung and other organs, ischemic heart disease and other circulatory diseases, and respiratory diseases such as emphysema. In regions where tuberculosis is prevalent, smokers also face a greater risk than nonsmokers of dying from this disease.

Since the poor are more likely to smoke than the rich, their risk of smoking-related and premature death is also greater. In high- and middle-income countries, men in the lowest socioeconomic groups are up to twice as likely to die in middle age as men in the highest socioeconomic groups, and smoking accounts for at least half their excess risk.

Smoking also affects the health of nonsmokers. Babies born to smoking mothers have lower birth weights, face greater risks of respiratory disease, and are more likely to die of sudden infant death syndrome than babies born to nonsmokers. Adult nonsmokers face small but increased risks of fatal and disabling disease from exposure to others' smoke.

Do smokers know their risks and bear their costs?

Modern economic theory holds that consumers are usually the best judges of how to spend their money on goods and services. This principle of consumer sovereignty is based on certain assumptions: first, that the consumer makes rational and informed choices after weighing the costs and benefits of purchases, and, second, that the consumer incurs all costs of the choice. When all consumers exercise their sovereignty in this way—knowing their risks and bearing their costs—then society's resources are, in theory, allocated as efficiently as possible. This report examines consumers' incentives to smoke, asks whether their choice to do so is like other consumption choices, and whether it results in an efficient allocation of society's resources, before discussing the implications for governments.

Smokers clearly perceive benefits from smoking, such as pleasure and the avoidance of withdrawal, and weigh these against the private costs of their choice. Defined this way, the perceived benefits outweigh the perceived costs, otherwise smokers would not pay to smoke. However, it appears that the choice to smoke may differ from the choice to buy other consumer goods in three specific ways.

First, there is evidence that many smokers are *not* fully aware of the high risks of disease and premature death that their choice entails. In low- and middle-income countries, many smokers may simply not know about these risks. In China in 1996, for example, 61 percent of smokers questioned thought that tobacco did them "little or no harm." In high-income countries, smokers know they face increased risks, but they judge the size of these risks to be lower and less well established than do nonsmokers, and they also minimize the personal relevance of these risks.

Second, smoking is usually started in adolescence or early adulthood. Even when they have been given information, young people do not always have the capacity to use it to make sound decisions. Young people may be less aware than adults of the risk to their health that smoking poses. Most new recruits and would-be smokers also underestimate the risk of becoming addicted to nicotine. As a result, they seriously underestimate the future costs of smoking—that is, the costs of being unable in later life to reverse a youthful decision to smoke. Societies generally recognize that adolescent decision-making capacity is limited, and restrict young people's freedom to make certain choices, for example, by denying them the right to vote or to marry until a certain age. Likewise, societies may consider it valid to restrict young people's freedom to choose to become addicted to smoking, a behavior that carries a much greater risk of eventual death than most other risky activities in which young people engage.

Third, smoking imposes costs on nonsmokers. With some of their costs borne by others, smokers may have an incentive to smoke more than they would if they were bearing all the costs themselves. The costs to nonsmokers clearly include health damage as well as nuisance and irritation from exposure to environmental tobacco smoke. In addition, smokers may impose financial costs on others. Such costs are more difficult to identify and quantify, and are variable in place and time, so it is not yet possible to determine how they might affect individuals' incentives to smoke more or less. However, we briefly discuss two such costs, healthcare and pensions.

In high-income countries, smoking-related healthcare accounts for between 6 and 15 percent of all annual healthcare costs. These figures will not necessarily apply to low- and middle-income countries, whose epidemics of smoking-related diseases are at earlier stages and may have other qualitative differences. Annual costs are of great importance to governments but, for individual consumers, the key question is the extent to which the costs will be borne by themselves or by others.

In any given year, smokers' healthcare costs will on average exceed nonsmokers'. If healthcare is paid for to some extent by general public taxation, nonsmokers will thus bear a part of the smoking population's costs. However, some analysts have argued that, because smokers tend to die earlier than nonsmokers, their *lifetime* healthcare costs may be no greater, and possibly even smaller, than nonsmokers'. This issue is controversial, but recent reviews in high-income countries suggest that smokers' lifetime costs are, after all, somewhat higher than nonsmokers', despite their shorter lives. However, whether higher or lower, the extent to which smokers impose their costs on others will depend on many factors, such as the existing level of cigarette taxes, and how much healthcare is provided by the public sector. In low- and middle-income countries, meanwhile, there have been no reliable studies of these issues.

The question of pensions is equally complex. Some analysts in high-income countries have argued that smokers "pay their way" by contributing to public pension schemes and then dying earlier, on average, than nonsmokers. However, this question is irrelevant to the low- and middle-income countries where most smokers live, because public pension coverage in these countries is low.

In sum, smokers certainly impose some physical costs, including health damage, nuisance, and irritation, on nonsmokers. They may also impose financial costs, but the scope of these is still unclear.

Appropriate responses

It appears unlikely, then, that most smokers either know their full risks or bear the full costs of their choice. Governments may consider that intervention is therefore justified, primarily to deter children and adolescents from smoking and to protect nonsmokers, but also to give adults all the information they need to make an informed choice.

Governments' interventions should ideally remedy each identified problem specifically. Thus, for example, children's imperfect judgments about the health effects of smoking would most specifically be addressed by improving their education and that of their parents, or by restricting their access to cigarettes. But adolescents respond poorly to health education, perfect parents are rare, and existing forms of restriction on cigarette sales to the young do not work, even in the high-income countries. In reality, the most effective way to deter children from taking up smoking is to increase taxes on tobacco. High prices prevent some children and adolescents from starting and encourage those who already smoke to reduce their consumption.

Taxation is a blunt instrument, however, and if taxes on cigarettes are raised, adult smokers will tend to smoke less and pay more for the cigarettes that they do purchase. In fulfilling the goal of protecting children and adolescents, taxation would thus also be imposing costs on adult smokers. These costs might, however, be considered acceptable, depending upon how much societies value curbing consumption in children. In any case, one long-term effect of reducing adult consumption may be to further discourage children and adolescents from smoking.

The problem of nicotine addiction would also need to be addressed. For established smokers who want to quit, the cost of withdrawal from nicotine is considerable. Governments might consider interventions to help reduce those costs as part of the overall tobacco control package.

Measures to reduce the demand for tobacco

We turn now to a discussion of measures for tobacco control, evaluating each in turn.

Raising taxes

Evidence from countries of all income levels shows that price increases on cigarettes are highly effective in reducing demand. Higher taxes induce some smokers to quit and prevent other individuals from starting. They also reduce the number of ex-smokers who return to cigarettes and reduce consumption among continuing smokers. On average, a price rise of 10 percent on a pack of cigarettes would be expected to reduce demand for cigarettes by about 4 percent in high-income countries and by about 8 percent in low- and middle-income countries, where lower incomes tend to make people more responsive to price changes. Children and adolescents are more responsive to price rises than older adults, so this intervention would have a significant impact on them.

Models for this report show that tax increases that would raise the real price of cigarettes by 10 percent worldwide would cause 40 million smokers alive in 1995 to quit, and prevent a minimum of 10 million tobacco-related deaths. The price rise would also deter others from taking up smoking in the first place. The assumptions on which the model is based are deliberately conservative, and these figures should therefore be regarded as minimum estimates.

As many policymakers are aware, the question of what the right level of tax should be is a complex one. The size of the tax depends in subtle ways on empirical facts that may not yet be available, such as the scale of the costs to nonsmokers and income levels. It also depends on varying societal values, such as the extent to which children should be protected, and on what a society hopes to achieve through the tax, such as a specific gain in revenue or a specific reduction in disease burden. The report concludes that, for the time being, policymakers who seek to reduce smoking should use as a yardstick the tax levels adopted as part of the comprehensive tobacco control policies of countries where cigarette consumption has fallen. In such countries, the tax component of the price of a pack of cigarettes is between two-thirds and four-fifths of the retail cost. Currently, in the high-income countries, taxes average about two-thirds or more of the retail price of a pack of cigarettes. In lower-income countries taxes amount to not more than half the retail price of a pack of cigarettes.

Nonprice measures to reduce demand

Beyond raising the price, governments have also employed a range of other effective measures. These include comprehensive bans on advertising and promotion of tobacco; information measures such as mass media counter-advertising, prominent health warning labels, the publication and dissemination of research findings on the health consequences of smoking as well as restrictions on smoking in work and public places.

This report provides evidence that each of these measures can reduce the demand for cigarettes. For example, "information shocks," such as the publication of research studies with significant new information on the health effects of smoking, reduce demand. Their effect appears to be greatest when a population has relatively little general awareness of the health risks. Comprehensive bans on advertising and promotion can reduce demand by around 7 percent, according to econometric studies in high-income countries. Smoking restrictions clearly benefit nonsmokers, and there is also some evidence that restrictions can reduce the prevalence of smoking.

Models developed for this report suggest that, employed as a package, such nonprice measures used globally could persuade some 23 million smokers alive in 1995 to quit and avert the tobacco-attributable deaths of 5 million of them. As with the estimates for tax increases, these are conservative estimates.

Nicotine replacement and other cessation therapies

A third intervention would be to help those who wish to quit by making it easier for them to obtain nicotine replacement therapy (NRT) and other cessation interventions. NRT markedly increases the effectiveness of cessation efforts and also reduces individuals' withdrawal costs. Yet in many countries, NRT is difficult to obtain. Models for this study suggest that if NRT were made more widely available, it could help to reduce demand substantially.

The combined effect of all these demand-reducing measures is not known, since smokers in most countries with tobacco control policies are exposed to a mixture of them and none can be studied strictly in isolation. However, there is evidence that the implementation of one intervention supports the success of others, underscoring the importance of implementing tobacco controls as a package. Together, in sum, these measures could avert many millions of deaths.

Measures to reduce the supply of tobacco

While interventions to reduce demand for tobacco are likely to succeed, measures to reduce its supply are less promising. This is because, if one supplier is shut down, an alternative supplier gains an incentive to enter the market.

The extreme measure of prohibiting tobacco is unwarranted on economic grounds as well as unrealistic and likely to fail. Crop substitution is often proposed as a means to reduce the tobacco supply, but there is scarcely any evidence that it reduces consumption, since the incentives to farmers to grow tobacco are currently much greater than for most other crops. While crop substitution is not an effective way to reduce consumption, it may be a useful strategy where needed to aid the poorest tobacco farmers in transition to other livelihoods, as part of a broader diversification program.

Similarly, the evidence so far suggests that trade restrictions, such as import bans, will have little impact on cigarette consumption worldwide. Instead, countries are more likely to succeed in curbing tobacco consumption by adopting measures that effectively reduce demand and applying those measures symmetrically to imported and domestically produced cigarettes. Likewise, in a framework of sound trade and agriculture policies, the subsidies on tobacco production that are found mainly in high-income countries make little sense. In any case, their removal would have little impact on total retail price.

However, one supply-side measure is key to an effective strategy for tobacco control: action against smuggling. Effective measures include prominent tax stamps and local-language warnings on cigarette packs, as well as the aggressive enforcement and consistent application of tough penalties to deter smugglers. Tight controls on smuggling improve governments' revenue yields from tobacco tax increases.

The costs and consequences of tobacco control

Policymakers traditionally raise several concerns about acting to control tobacco. The first of these concerns is that tobacco controls will cause permanent job losses in an economy. However, falling demand for tobacco does not mean a fall in a country's total employment level. Money that smokers once spent on cigarettes would instead be spent on other goods and services, generating other jobs to replace any lost from the tobacco industry. Studies for this report show that most countries would see no net job losses, and that a few would see net gains, if tobacco consumption fell.

There are however a very small number of countries, mostly in Sub-Saharan Africa, whose economies are heavily dependent on tobacco farming. For these countries, while reductions in domestic demand would have little impact, a global fall in demand would result in job losses. Policies to aid adjustment in such circumstances would be essential. However, it should be stressed that, even if demand were to fall significantly, it would occur slowly, over a generation or more.

A second concern is that higher tax rates will reduce government revenues. In fact, the empirical evidence shows that raised tobacco taxes bring greater tobacco tax revenues. This is in part because the proportionate reduction in demand does not match the proportionate size of the tax increase, since addicted consumers respond relatively slowly to price rises. A model developed for this study concludes that modest increases in cigarette excise taxes of

10 percent worldwide would increase tobacco tax revenues by about 7 percent overall, with the effects varying by country.

A third concern is that higher taxes will lead to massive increases in smuggling, thereby keeping cigarette consumption high but reducing government revenues. Smuggling is a serious problem, but the report concludes that, even where it occurs at high rates, tax increases bring greater revenues and reduce consumption. Therefore, rather than foregoing tax increases, the appropriate response to smuggling is to crack down on criminal activity.

A fourth concern is that increases in cigarette taxes will have a disproportionate impact on poor consumers. Existing tobacco taxes do consume a higher share of the income of poor consumers than of rich consumers. However, policymakers' main concern should be over the distributional impact of the entire tax and expenditure system, and less on particular taxes in isolation. It is important to note that poor consumers are usually more responsive to price increases than rich consumers, so their consumption of cigarettes will fall more sharply following a tax increase, and their relative *financial* burden may be correspondingly reduced. Nonetheless, their loss of perceived benefits of smoking may be comparatively greater.

Is tobacco control worth paying for?

For governments considering intervention, an important further consideration is the cost-effectiveness of tobacco control measures relative to other health interventions. Preliminary estimates were performed for this report in which the public costs of implementing tobacco control programs were weighed against the potential number of healthy years of life saved. The results are consistent with earlier studies that suggest that tobacco control is highly cost-effective as part of a basic public health package in low- and middle-income countries.

Measured in terms of the cost per year of healthy life saved, tax increases would be cost-effective. Depending on various assumptions, this instrument could cost between US$5 and $17[1] for each year of healthy life saved in low- and middle-income countries. This compares favorably with many health interventions commonly financed by governments, such as child immunization. Nonprice measures are also cost-effective in many settings. Measures to liberalize access to nicotine replacement therapy, for example, by changing the conditions for its sale, would probably also be cost-effective in most settings. However, individual countries would need to make careful assessments before deciding to provide subsidies for NRT and other cessation interventions for poor smokers.

The unique potential of tobacco taxation to raise revenues cannot be ignored. In China, for example, conservative estimates suggest that a 10 percent increase in cigarette tax would decrease consumption by 5 percent, increase revenue by 5 percent, and that the increase would be sufficient to finance a package of essential health services for one-third of China's poorest 100 million citizens.

An agenda for action

Each society makes its own decisions about policies that concern individual choices. In reality, most policies would be based on a mix of criteria, not only economic ones. Most societies would wish to reduce the unquantifiable suffering and emotional losses wrought by tobacco's burden of disease and premature death. For the policymaker seeking to improve public health, too, tobacco control is an attractive option. Even modest reductions in a disease burden of such large size would bring highly significant health gains.

Some policymakers will consider that the strongest grounds for intervening are to deter children from smoking. However, a strategy aimed solely at deterring children is not practical and would bring no significant benefits to public health for several decades. Most of the tobacco-related deaths that are projected to occur in the next 50 years are among today's existing smokers. Governments concerned with health gains in the medium term may therefore consider adopting broader measures that also help adults to quit.

The report has two recommendations:

1. Where **governments** decide to take strong action to curb the tobacco epidemic, a multi-pronged strategy should be adopted. Its aims should be to deter children from smoking, to protect nonsmokers, and to provide all smokers with information about the health effects of tobacco. The strategy, tailored to individual country needs, would include: (1) raising taxes, using as a yardstick the rates adopted by countries with comprehensive tobacco control policies where consumption has fallen. In these countries, tax accounts for two-thirds to four-fifths of the retail price of cigarettes; (2) publishing and disseminating research results on the health effects of tobacco, adding prominent warning labels to cigarettes, adopting comprehensive bans on advertising and promotion, and restricting smoking in workplaces and public places; and (3) widening access to nicotine replacement and other cessation therapies.
2. **International organizations such as the UN agencies** should review their existing programs and policies to ensure that tobacco control is given due prominence; they should sponsor research into the causes, consequences, and costs of smoking, and the cost-effectiveness of interventions at the local level; and they should address tobacco control

issues that cross borders, including working with the WHO's proposed Framework Convention for Tobacco Control. Key areas for action include facilitating international agreements on smuggling control, discussions on tax harmonization to reduce the incentives for smuggling, and bans on advertising and promotion involving the global communications media.

The threat posed by smoking to global health is unprecedented, but so is the potential for reducing smoking-related mortality with cost-effective policies. This report shows the scale of what might be achieved: moderate action could ensure substantial health gains for the 21st century.

Note

1. All dollar amounts are current U.S. dollars.

CHAPTER 1

Global Trends in Tobacco Use

ALTHOUGH people have used tobacco for centuries, cigarettes did not appear in mass-manufactured form until the 19th century. Since then, the practice of cigarette smoking has spread worldwide on a massive scale. Today, about one in three adults, or 1.1 billion people, smoke. Of these, about 80 percent live in low- and middle-income countries. Partly because of growth in the adult population, and partly because of increased consumption, the total number of smokers is expected to reach about 1.6 billion by 2025.

In the past, tobacco was often chewed, or smoked in various kinds of pipes. While these practices persist, they are declining. Manufactured cigarettes 0and various types of hand-rolled cigarette such as *bidis*—common in southeast Asia and India—now account for up to 85 percent of all tobacco consumed worldwide. Cigarette smoking appears to pose much greater dangers to health than earlier forms of tobacco use. This report therefore focuses on manufactured cigarettes and *bidis*.

Rising consumption in low-income and middle-income countries

The populations of the low- and middle-income countries have been increasing their cigarette consumption since about 1970 (see Figure 1.1). The per capita consumption in these countries climbed steadily between 1970 and 1990, although the upward trend may have slowed a little since the early 1990s.

FIGURE 1.1   SMOKING IS INCREASING IN THE DEVELOPING WORLD
Trends in per capita adult cigarette consumption

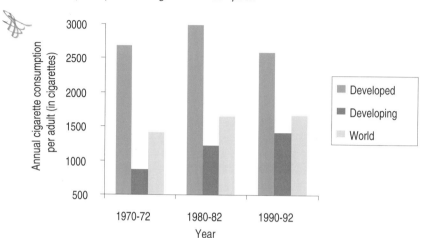

Source: World Health Organization. 1997. *Tobacco or Health: a Global Status Report.*
Geneva, Switzerland.

While the practice of smoking has become more prevalent among men in low- and middle-income countries, it has been in overall decline among men in the high-income countries during the same period. For example, more than 55 percent of men in the United States smoked at the peak of consumption in the mid-20th century, but the proportion had fallen to 28 percent by the mid-1990s. Per capita consumption for the populations of the high-income countries as a whole also has dropped. However, among certain groups in these countries, such as teenagers and young women, the proportion who smoke has grown in the 1990s. Overall, then, the smoking epidemic is spreading from its original focus, among men in high-income countries, to women in high-income countries and men in low-income regions.

In recent years, international trade agreements have liberalized global trade in many goods and services. Cigarettes are no exception. The removal of trade barriers tends to introduce greater competition that results in lower prices, greater advertising and promotion, and other activities that stimulate demand. One study concluded that, in four Asian economies that opened their markets in response to U.S. trade pressure during the 1980s—Japan, South Korea, Taiwan, and Thailand—consumption of cigarettes per person was almost 10 percent higher in 1991 than it would have been if these markets had remained closed. An econometric model developed for this report concludes that increased trade liberalization contributed significantly to increases in cigarette consumption, particularly in the low- and middle-income countries.

Regional patterns in smoking

Data on the number of smokers in each region have been compiled by the World Health Organization using more than 80 separate studies. For the purpose of this report, these data have been used to estimate the prevalence of smoking in each of the seven World Bank country groupings.[1] As Table 1.1 shows, there are wide variations between regions and, in particular, in the prevalence of smoking among women in different regions. For example, in Eastern Europe and Central Asia (mainly the former socialist economies), 59 percent of men and 26 percent of women smoked in 1995, more than in any other region. Yet in East Asia and the Pacific, where the prevalence of male smoking is equally high, at 59 percent, just 4 percent of women were smokers.

Smoking and socioeconomic status

Historically, as incomes rose within populations, the number of people who smoked rose too. In the earlier decades of the smoking epidemic in high-income countries, smokers were more likely to be affluent than poor. But in the

TABLE 1.1 REGIONAL PATTERNS OF SMOKING
Estimated smoking prevalence by gender and number of smokers in population aged 15 or more, by World Bank region, 1995

World Bank	Smoking prevalence (%)			Total smokers	(% of all
Region	Males	Females	Overall	(millions)	smokers)
East Asia and Pacific	59	4	32	401	35
Eastern Europe and Central Asia	59	26	41	148	13
Latin America and Caribbean	40	21	30	95	8
Middle East and North Africa	44	5	25	40	3
South Asia (cigarettes)	20	1	11	86	8
South Asia (bidis)	20	3	12	96	8
Sub-Saharan Africa	33	10	21	67	6
Low/Middle Income	49	9	29	933	82
High Income	39	22	30	209	18
World	47	12	29	1,142	100

*Note:*Numbers have been rounded.
Source: Author's calculations based on World Health Organization. 1997. *Tobacco or health: a Global Status Report.* Geneva, Switzerland.

past three to four decades, this pattern appears to have been reversed, at least among men, for whom data are widely available.[2] Affluent men in the high-income countries have increasingly abandoned tobacco, whereas poorer men have not done so. For example, in Norway, the percentage of men with high incomes who smoked fell from 75 percent in 1955 to 28 percent in 1990. Over the same period, the proportion of men on low incomes who smoked declined much less steeply, from 60 percent in 1955 to 48 percent in 1990. Today, in most high-income countries, there are significant differences in the prevalence of smoking between different socioeconomic groups. In the United Kingdom, for instance, only 10 percent of women and 12 percent of men in the highest socioeconomic group are smokers; in the lowest socioeconomic groups the corresponding figures are threefold greater: 35 percent and 40 percent. The same inverse relationship is found between education levels—a marker for socioeconomic status—and smoking. In general, individuals who have received little or no education are more likely to smoke than those who are more educated.

Until recently, it was thought that the situation in low- and middle-income countries was different. However, the most recent research concludes that here too, men of low socioeconomic status are more likely to smoke than those of high socioeconomic status. Educational level is a clear determinant of smoking in Chennai, India (Figure 1.2). Studies in Brazil, China, South Africa, Vietnam, and several Central American nations confirm this pattern.

While it is thus clear that the *prevalence* of smoking is higher among the poor and less educated worldwide, there are fewer data on the *number of cigarettes smoked* daily by different socioeconomic groups. In high-income countries, with some exceptions, poor and less educated men smoke more cigarettes per day than richer, more educated men. While it might have been expected that poor men in low- and middle-income countries would smoke fewer cigarettes than affluent men, the available data indicate that, in general, smokers with low levels of education consume equal or slightly larger numbers of cigarettes than those with high levels of education. An important exception is India, where, not surprisingly, smokers with college-level education status tend to consume more cigarettes, which are relatively more expensive, while smokers with low levels of education status consume larger numbers of the inexpensive *bidis*.

Age and the uptake of smoking

It is unlikely that individuals who avoid starting to smoke in adolescence or young adulthood will ever become smokers. Nowadays, the overwhelming majority of smokers start before age 25, often in childhood or adolescence (see Box 1.1 and Figure 1.3); in the high-income countries, eight out of 10

FIGURE 1.2 SMOKING IS MORE COMMON AMONG THE LESS EDUCATED
Smoking prevalence among men in Chennai (India) by education levels

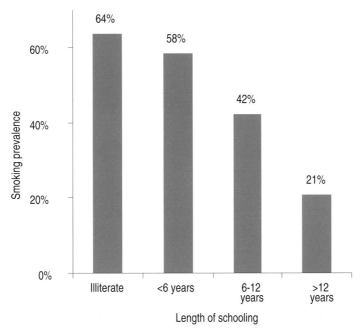

Source: Gajalakshmi, C. K., P. Jha, S. Nguyen, and A. Yurekli. *Patterns of Tobacco Use, and Health Consequences.* Background paper.

begin in their teens. In middle-income and low-income countries for which data are available, it appears that most smokers start by the early twenties, but the trend is toward younger ages. For example, in China between 1984 and 1996, there was a significant increase in the number of young men aged between 15 and 19 years who took up smoking. A similar decline in the age of starting has been observed in the high-income countries.

Global patterns of quitting

While there is evidence that smoking begins in youth worldwide, the proportion of smokers who quit appears to vary sharply between high-income countries and the rest of the world, at least to date. In environments of steadily

FIGURE 1.3   SMOKING STARTS EARLY IN LIFE
Cumulative distribution of smoking initiation age in China, India, and the United States

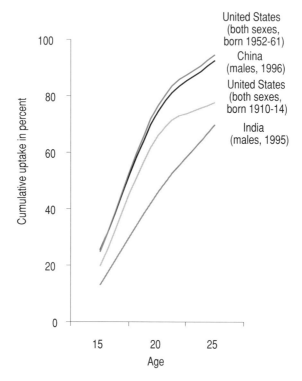

Sources: Chinese Academy of Preventive Medicine. 1997. *Smoking in China: 1996 National Prevalence Survey of Smoking Pattern.* Beijing. Science and Technology Press; Gupta, P.C., 1996. "Survey of Sociodemographic Characteristics of Tobacco Use Among 99,598 Individuals in Bombay, India, Using Handheld Computers." *Tobacco Control* 5:114–20, and U. S. Surgeon General Reports, 1989 and 1994.

increased knowledge about the health effects of tobacco, the prevalence of smoking has gradually fallen, and a significant number of former smokers have accumulated over the decades. In most high-income countries, about 30 percent of the male population are former smokers. In contrast, only 2 percent of Chinese men had quit in 1993, only 5 percent of Indian males at around the same period, and only 10 percent of Vietnamese males had quit in 1997.

BOX 1.1   HOW MANY YOUNG PEOPLE TAKE UP SMOKING EACH DAY?

Individuals who start to smoke at a young age are likely to become heavy smokers, and are also at increased risk of dying from smoking-related diseases in later life. It is therefore important to know how many children and young people take up smoking daily. We attempt here to answer this question.

We used (1) World Bank data on the number of children and adolescents, male and female, who reached age 20 in 1995, for each World Bank region, and (2) data from the World Health Organization on the prevalence of smokers in all age groups up to the age of 30 in each of these regions. For an upper estimate, we assumed that the number of young people who take up smoking every day is a product of 1*2 per region, for each gender. For a lower estimate, we reduced this by region-specific estimates for the number of smokers who start after the age of 30.

We made three conservative assumptions: first, that there have been minimal changes over time in the average age of uptake. There have been recent downward trends in the age of uptake in young Chinese men, but assuming little change means that, if anything, our figures are underestimates. Second, we focused on regular smokers, excluding the much larger number of children who would try smoking but not become regular smokers. Third, we assumed that, for those young people who become regular smokers, quitting before adulthood is rare. While the number of adolescent regular smokers who quit is substantial in high-income countries, in low- and middle-income countries it is currently very low.

With these assumptions, we calculated that the number of children and young people taking up smoking ranges from 14,000 to 15,000 per day in the high-income countries as a whole. For middle- and low-income countries, the estimated numbers range from 68,000 to 84,000. This means that every day, worldwide, there are between 82,000 and 99,000 young people starting to smoke and risking rapid addiction to nicotine. These figures are consistent with existing estimates for individual high-income countries.

Notes

1. These groupings are shown in Appendix D. In sum, they are as follows: (1) East Asia and the Pacific, (2) Eastern Europe and Central Asia (a group that includes most of the former socialist economies), (3) the Middle East and North Africa, (4) Latin American and the Caribbean, (5) South Asia, (6) Sub-Saharan Africa, and (7) the high-income countries, broadly equivalent to the members of the Organization for Economic Cooperation and Development (OECD).

2. Research into women's smoking patterns is much more limited. Where women have been smoking for decades, the relationship between socioeconomic status and smoking is similar to that seen in men, Elsewhere, more reliable information is needed before conclusions can be drawn.

CHAPTER 2

The Health Consequences of Smoking

THE impact of tobacco on health has been extensively documented. This report does not seek to repeat this information in detail but simply to summarize the evidence. The section is divided into two parts: first, a brief discussion of nicotine addiction; and second, a description of the disease burden attributable to tobacco.

The addictive nature of tobacco smoking

Tobacco contains nicotine, a substance that is recognized to be addictive by international medical organizations. Tobacco dependence is listed in the International Classification of Diseases. Nicotine fulfills the key criteria for addiction or dependence, including compulsive use, despite the desire and repeated attempts to quit; psychoactive effects produced by the action of the substance on the brain; and behavior motivated by the "reinforcing" effects of the psychoactive substance. Cigarettes, unlike chewed tobacco, enable nicotine to reach the brain rapidly, within a few seconds of inhaling smoke, and the smoker can regulate the dose puff by puff.

Nicotine addiction can be established quickly. In young adolescents who have recently taken up smoking, saliva concentrations of cotinine, a breakdown product of nicotine, climb steeply over time toward the levels found in established smokers (Figure 2.1). The average levels of nicotine inhaled are sufficient to have a pharmacological effect and to play a role in reinforcing smoking. Yet many young smokers underestimate their risks of becoming addicted. Between half and three-quarters of young smokers in the United States say they have tried to quit at least once and failed. Surveys in the high-income countries

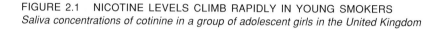

FIGURE 2.1   NICOTINE LEVELS CLIMB RAPIDLY IN YOUNG SMOKERS
Saliva concentrations of cotinine in a group of adolescent girls in the United Kingdom

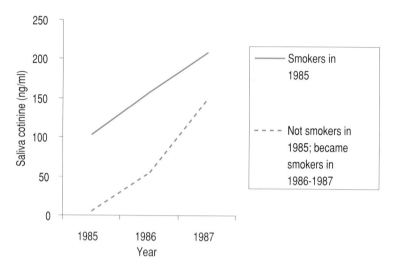

Source: McNeill, A. D. and others. 1989. "Nicotine Intake in Young Smokers: Longitudinal Study of Saliva Cotinine Concentrations." *American Journal of Public Health* 79(2): 172–75.

suggest that a substantial proportion of smokers as young as 16 regret their use of cigarettes but feel unable to stop.

It is of course possible to abstain permanently, as is the case with other addictive substances. However, without cessation interventions, the individual success rates are low. The most recent research concludes that, of regular smokers who try to quit unaided, 98 percent will have started again within a year.

The disease burden

Within the next year, tobacco is expected to kill approximately 4 million people worldwide. Already, it is responsible for one in 10 adult deaths; by 2030 the figure is expected to be one in six, or 10 million deaths each year—more than any other cause and more than the projected death tolls from pneumonia, diarrheal diseases, tuberculosis, and the complications of childbirth for that year *combined*. If current trends persist, about 500 million people alive today will eventually be killed by tobacco, half of them in productive middle age, losing 20 to 25 years of life.

Smoking-related deaths, once largely confined to men in the high-income countries, are now spreading to women in high-income countries and men throughout the world (Table 2.1). Whereas in 1990 two out of every three smoking-related deaths were in either the high-income countries or the former socialist states of Eastern Europe and Central Asia, by 2030, seven out of every 10 such deaths will be in low- and middle-income countries. Of the half-billion deaths expected among people alive today, about 100 million will be in Chinese men.

Long delays between exposure and disease

However, the toll of death and disability from smoking outside the high-income countries has yet to be felt. This is because the diseases caused by smoking can take several decades to develop. Even when smoking is very common in a population, the damage to health may not yet be visible. This point can be most clearly demonstrated by trends in lung cancer in the United States. While the most rapid growth in cigarette consumption in the United States happened between 1915 and 1950, rates of lung cancer did not begin to rise steeply until about 1945. Age-standardized rates of the disease trebled between the 1930s and 1950s, but after 1955 the rates increased much more: by the 1980s, rates were *11-fold* higher than levels in 1940.

In China today, where one-quarter of the world's smokers live, cigarette consumption is as high as it was in the United States in 1950, when per capita consumption levels were reaching their peak. At that stage of the U.S. epidemic, tobacco was responsible for 12 percent of all the nation's deaths in middle age. Forty years later, when cigarette consumption in the United States was already in decline, tobacco was responsible for about *one-third* of the nation's middle-aged deaths. Today, in a striking echo of the U.S. experience, tobacco is estimated to be responsible for about 12 percent of male middle-aged deaths in China. Researchers expect that within a few decades, the proportion there will rise to about one in three, as it did in the United States. In

TABLE 2.1   CURRENT AND ESTIMATED FUTURE DEATHS FROM TOBACCO (millions per year)

	Number of tobacco deaths in 2000	*Number of tobacco deaths projected for 2030*
Developed	2	3
Developing	2	7

Source: World Health Organization. 1999. *Making a Difference*. World Health Report. 1999. Geneva, Switzerland.

contrast, smoking among young Chinese women has not increased markedly in the past two decades, and most of those women who do smoke are older. Thus, on current smoking patterns, female tobacco-attributable deaths in China may actually drop from their current level of about 2 percent of the total to less than 1 percent.

Even in the high-income countries whose populations have been exposed to smoking for many decades, a clear picture of tobacco-related diseases has taken at least 40 years to emerge. Researchers calculate the excess risk of death in smokers through prospective studies that compare the health outcomes of smokers and nonsmokers. After 20 years of follow-up, in the early 1970s, researchers believed that smokers faced a one-in-four risk of being killed by tobacco, but now, with more data, they believe that the risk is one in two.

How smoking kills

In the high-income countries, long-term prospective studies such as the American Cancer Society's Second Cancer Prevention study, which followed more than 1 million U.S. adults, have provided reliable evidence of how smoking kills. Smokers in the United States are 20 times more likely to die of lung cancer in middle age than nonsmokers and three times more likely to die in middle age of vascular diseases, including heart attacks, strokes, and other diseases of the arteries or veins. Because ischemic heart disease is common in high-income countries, the smoker's excess risk translates into a very large number of deaths, making heart disease the most common smoking-related cause of death in these countries. Smoking is also the leading cause of chronic bronchitis and emphysema. It is associated with cancers of various other organs, including the bladder, kidney, larynx, mouth, pancreas, and stomach.

A person's risk of developing lung cancer is affected more strongly by the amount of time that they have been a smoker than by the number of cigarettes they have smoked daily. Put differently, a threefold increase in the duration of smoking is associated with a 100-fold risk of lung cancer, whereas a threefold increase in the number of cigarettes smoked each day is associated with only a threefold risk of lung cancer. Thus those who start to smoke in their teens and who continue face the biggest risks.

For some years, cigarette manufacturers have marketed certain brands as "low tar" and "low nicotine," a modification that many smokers believe makes cigarettes safer. However, the difference in the risk of premature death for smokers of low-tar or low-nicotine brands compared with smokers of ordinary cigarettes is far less than the difference in risk between nonsmokers and smokers.

The epidemic varies in place as well as in time

Because most long-term studies have been confined to the high-income countries, data on the health effects of tobacco elsewhere have been scant. However,recent major studies from China, and emerging studies from India, indicate that although the overall risks of persistent smoking are about as great as in high-income countries such as the United States and the United Kingdom, the pattern of smoking-related diseases in these nations is substantially different. The data from China suggest that deaths from ischemic heart disease make up a much smaller proportion of the total number of deaths caused by tobacco than in the West, while respiratory diseases and cancers account for most of the deaths. Strikingly, a significant minority involve tuberculosis. Other differences may emerge in other populations; for instance, in South Asia, the pattern may be affected by a high underlying prevalence of cardiovascular disease. These results underscore the importance of monitoring the epidemic in all regions. Nevertheless, despite the different patterns of smoking-related disease in different populations, it appears that the overall *proportion* who are eventually killed by persistent cigarette smoking is generally about one in two in many populations.

Smoking and the health disadvantage of the poor

As tobacco use is associated with poverty and low socioeconomic status, so are its damaging effects on health. Analyses for this report show the impact of smoking on the survival of men in different socioeconomic groups (measured by income, social class, or educational level) in four countries where the smoking epidemic is mature—Canada, Poland, the United Kingdom, and the United States.

In Poland in 1996 men with a university education had a 26 percent risk of death in middle age. For men with only primary-level education, the risk was 52 percent—twice as great. By analyzing the proportion of deaths due to smoking in each group, researchers estimate that tobacco is responsible for about two-thirds of the *excess* risk in the group with only primary-level education. In other words, if smoking were eliminated, the survival gap between the two groups would narrow sharply. The risk of death in middle age would fall to 28 percent in men with only primary-level education and 20 percent in those with university education (Figure 2. 2) . Similar results emerge from the other countries in the study, indicating that tobacco is responsible for more than half of the difference in adult male mortality between those of highest and lowest socioeconomic status in these countries. Smoking has also contributed heavily to the widening of the survival gap over time between affluent and disadvantaged men in these countries (Figure 2.3).

The risks from others' smoke

FIGURE 2.2   EDUCATION AND THE RISK OF SMOKING-
ATTRIBUTABLE DEATH
Deaths in middle-aged males of different education levels, Poland 1996

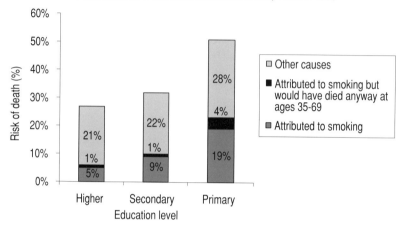

Note: Numbers have been rounded.
Source: Bobak, Martin, P. Jha, M. Jarvis, and S. Nguyen. *Poverty and Tobacco.* Background paper.

Smokers affect not only their own health but the health of those around them.
Women who smoke during pregnancy are more likely to lose the fetus through
spontaneous abortion. Babies born to smoking mothers in high-income countries are significantly more likely than the babies of nonsmokers to have a low
birth weight and up to 35 percent more likely to die in infancy. They also face
higher risks of respiratory disease. Recent research has shown that a carcino-
gen found only in tobacco smoke is present in the urine of newborn babies
born to smokers.

Cigarette smoking accounts for much of the health disadvantage of babies
born to poorer women. Among white women in the United States, smoking
alone has been found to be responsible for 63 percent of the difference in birth
weight between babies born to college-educated women and babies born to
those who received a high school education or less.

Adults exposed chronically to others' tobacco smoke also face small but
real risks of lung cancer and higher risks of cardiovascular disease, while the
children of smokers suffer a range of health problems and functional limita-
tions.

FIGURE 2.3 SMOKING AND THE WIDENING HEALTH GAP BETWEEN THE RICH AND THE POOR
Smoking and difference in the risks of death in middle-aged men between higher and lower socioeconomic status (SES) in the United Kingdom

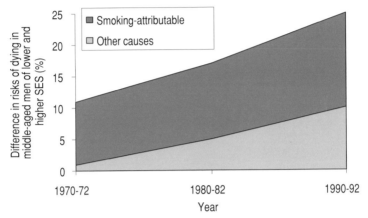

Note: In the U.K., socioeconomic status is categorized into five groups from I (the highest) to V (the lowest). This figure examines the difference in the risks of dying among middle-aged men of groups I and II versus group V over time.
Source: Bobak, Martin, P. Jha, M. Jarvis, and S. Nguyen. *Poverty and Tobacco.* Background paper.

Nonsmokerswho are exposed to smoke include the children and the spouses of smokers, mostly within their own homes. Also, a substantial number of nonsmokers work with smokers, or in smoky environments, where their exposure over time is significant.

Quitting works

The earlier a smoker starts, the greater the risk of disabling illnesses. In high-income countries with long-term data, researchers have concluded that smokers who start early and smoke regularly are much more likely to develop lung cancer than smokers who quit while they are still young. In the United Kingdom, male doctors who stop smoking before the age of 35 survive about as well as those who never smoked. Those who quit between the ages of 35 and 44 also gain substantial benefits, and there are benefits at older ages, too.

In sum, then, the epidemic of smoking-related disease is expanding from its original focus in men in high-income countries to affect women in high-income countries and men in low- and middle-income countries. Smoking is increasingly associated with social disadvantage, as measured by income and educational levels. Most new smokers underestimate the risk of becoming addicted to nicotine; by early adulthood, many regret starting to smoke and feel unable to stop. Half of long-term smokers will eventually be killed by tobacco, and half of these will die in middle age.

CHAPTER 3

Do Smokers Know Their Risks and
Bear Their Costs?

In this chapter, we examine the incentives for people to smoke. We consider whether smoking is like other consumption choices, and whether it results in an efficient allocation of society's resources. We then discuss the implications for governments.

Modern economic theory holds that individual consumers are the best judges of how to spend their money on goods such as rice, clothing, or movies. This principle of consumer sovereignty is based on certain assumptions: first, that each consumer makes rational and informed choices after weighing the costs and benefits of purchases, and, second, that the consumer incurs all costs of the choice. When all consumers exercise their sovereignty in this way—knowing their risks and bearing the costs of their choices—then society's resources are, in theory, allocated as efficiently as possible.

Smokers clearly perceive benefits from smoking; otherwise they would not pay to do it. The perceived benefits include pleasure and satisfaction, enhanced self-image, stress control and, for the addicted smoker, the avoidance of nicotine withdrawal. The private costs to be weighed against those benefits include money spent on tobacco products, damage to health, and nicotine addiction. Defined this way, the perceived benefits evidently outweigh the perceived costs.

However, the choice to buy tobacco products differs in three specific ways from the choice to buy other consumer goods:

- First, there is evidence that many smokers are *not* fully aware of the high probability of disease and premature death that their choice entails. This is the major private cost of smoking.

■ Second, there is evidence that children and teenagers may not have the capacity to properly assess any information that they possess about the health effects of smoking. Equally important, there is evidence that new recruits to smoking may seriously underestimate the future costs associated with addiction to nicotine. These future costs may be thought of as the costs for adult smokers of being unable to alter a youthful decision to smoke, even if desired, because of addiction.

■ Third, there is evidence that smokers impose costs on other individuals, both directly and indirectly. Economists usually assume that individuals properly weigh the costs and benefits of their choices only when they themselves incur these costs and enjoy these benefits. If others bear some of the costs, it follows that smokers may smoke more than they would if they were bearing all the costs themselves.

We consider the evidence for each of these in turn.

Awareness of the risks

People's knowledge of the health risks of smoking appears to be partial at best, especially in low- and middle-income countries where information about these hazards is limited. In China, for example, 61 percent of adult smokers surveyed in 1996 believed that cigarettes did them "little or no harm."

In the high-income countries, general awareness of the health effects of smoking has undoubtedly increased over the past four decades. However, there has been much controversy about how accurately smokers in high-income countries perceive their risks of developing disease. Various studies conducted over the past two decades have produced mixed conclusions about the accuracy of individuals' perceptions of the risks from smoking. Some find that people overstate these risks, others find that the risks are underestimated, and still others find that risk perceptions are adequate. The methodologies employed in these studies, however, have been criticized on multiple grounds. An overview of the research literature recently concluded that smokers in high-income countries are generally aware of their increased risks of disease, but that they judge the size of these risks to be smaller and less well-established than do nonsmokers. Moreover, even where individuals have a reasonably accurate perception of the health risks faced by smokers *as a group*, they minimize the personal relevance of this information, believing other smokers' risks to be greater than their own.

Finally, there is evidence from various countries that some smokers may have a distorted perception of the health risks of smoking compared with other health risks. For example, in Poland in 1995 researchers asked adults to rate "the most important factors influencing human health." The factor most frequently chosen was "the environment," followed by "dietary habits" and "stress or hectic lifestyles." Smoking trailed in fourth place, and was mentioned by only 27 percent of adults questioned. In fact, smoking accounts for more than one-third of the risk of premature death in middle-aged men in Poland, far more than any other risk factor.

Youth, addiction, and the capacity to make sound decisions

As stated in chapter 1, most smoking starts early in life, and children and teenagers may know less about the health effects of smoking than adults. A recent survey of 15- and 16-year-olds in Moscow found that more than half either knew of no smoking-related diseases or could name only one, lung cancer. Even in the United States, where young people might be expected to have received more information, almost half of 13-year-olds today think that smoking a pack of cigarettes a day will not cause them great harm. Given adolescents' inadequate knowledge, they face greater obstacles than adults in making informed choices.

Equally important, young people underestimate the risk of becoming addicted to nicotine, and therefore grossly underestimate their future costs from smoking. Among final-year high school students in the United States who smoke but believe they will quit within five years, fewer than two out of five actually do quit. The rest are still smoking five years later. In high-income countries, about seven out of 10 adult smokers say they regret their choice to start smoking. Using econometric models of the relationship between current smoking and past smoking, based on U.S. data, researchers estimate that addiction to nicotine accounts for at least 60 percent of the cigarette consumption in any one year, and possibly as much as 95 percent.

Even teenagers who have been told about the risks of smoking may have a limited capacity to use the information wisely. It is difficult for most teenagers to imagine being 25, let alone 55, and warnings about the damage that smoking will inflict on their health at some distant date are unlikely to reduce their desire to smoke. The risk that young people will make unwise decisions is recognized by most societies and is not unique to choices about smoking. Most societies restrict young people's power to make certain decisions, although these vary from culture to culture. For example, most democracies prevent their young people from voting before a certain age; some societies make education compulsory up to a certain age; and many prevent marriage before a certain age. The consensus across most societies is that some decisions are best left until adulthood. Likewise, societies may consider that the freedom of young people to choose to become addicted should be restricted.

It might be argued that young people are attracted to many risky behaviors, such as fast driving or alcohol binge-drinking, and that there is nothing special about smoking. However, there are several differences. First, for most of the world, smoking is less heavily regulated than other risky behaviors. Drivers are usually penalized for excessive speed with heavy fines and even loss of license, and there are penalties for dangerous behavior associated with heavy drinking, such as drunk driving. Second, smoking is much more dangerous than most risky activities over a lifetime. Extrapolations based on data from high-income countries suggest that, of 1,000 15-year-old males currently living in low- and middle-income countries, 125 will be killed by smoking in middle age if they continue to smoke regularly, with an additional 125 in old age. By comparison, about 10 will die in middle age due to road accidents, about 10 will die in middle age because of violence, and about 30 will die in middle age of alcohol-related causes, including some road accidents and violent deaths. Third, few other risky behaviors carry the high risk of addiction that is seen with smoking, so most are easier to abandon, and are abandoned, in maturity.

Costs imposed on others

Smokers impose physical costs on others as well as possible financial costs. In theory, smokers would smoke less if they took these costs into account, because the socially optimal level of consumption, in which resources are efficiently distributed in society, is reached when all costs are borne by the consumer. If part of the costs are borne by nonsmokers, then cigarette consumption may be higher than socially optimal. We now briefly discuss the various types of costs imposed on others.

First, smokers impose direct health costs on nonsmokers. The health effects, described in chapter 2, include low birth weight and increased risk of various diseases in the infants of smoking mothers, and disease in children and adults chronically exposed to second-hand smoke. Other direct costs include irritation and nuisance from smoke and the cost of cleaning clothes and furnishings. Although evidence is much more patchy, there may also be a cost from fires, environmental degradation, and deforestation from tobacco growing and processing, and from the consequences of smoking.

Given existing data, the financial costs that smokers impose on others are difficult to identify and quantify. This report does not attempt to provide an estimate of these costs, but instead it describes some of the main areas in which such costs can arise. We first discuss the cost of healthcare for smokers, then the issue of pensions.

In high-income countries, the overall annual cost of healthcare that may be attributed to smoking has been estimated to be between 6 and 15 percent of total healthcare costs. In most low- and middle-income countries today, the annual costs of healthcare attributable to smoking are lower than this, partly because the epidemic of tobacco-related diseases is at an earlier stage, and partly because of other factors such as the kinds of tobacco-related diseases that are most prevalent and the treatments that they require. However, these countries are likely to see their annual smoking-related healthcare costs rise in the future. Projections performed for this report for China and India suggest that the annual costs of healthcare for smoking-related disease will grow to absorb a larger percentage of gross domestic product (GDP) than today.

For policymakers, it is vital to know these annual healthcare costs and the fraction borne by the public sector, because they represent real resources that cannot be used for other goods and services. For individual consumers, on the other hand, the key issue is the extent to which the costs will be borne by themselves or by others. Again, if some of the costs are likely to be borne by nonsmokers, consumers have an incentive to smoke more than they would if they were expecting to bear all the costs themselves. As the following discussion shows, however, the assessment of these costs is complex, and therefore it is not yet possible to conclude anything about how they may influence smokers' consumption choices.

In any given year, on average, a smoker's healthcare is likely to cost more than that of a nonsmoker of the same age and sex. However, because smokers tend to die earlier than nonsmokers, the *lifetime* healthcare costs of smokers and nonsmokers in high-income countries may be fairly similar. Studies that measure the lifetime healthcare costs of smokers and nonsmokers in the high-income countries have reached conflicting conclusions. In the Netherlands and Switzerland, for example, smokers and nonsmokers have been found to have similar costs, while in the United Kingdom and the United States some studies have concluded that smokers' lifetime costs are in fact higher. Recent reviews that take account of the growing number of tobacco-attributable diseases and other factors conclude that, overall, smokers' lifetime costs in high-income countries are somewhat greater than those of nonsmokers, despite their earlier deaths. There are no such reliable studies on lifetime healthcare costs in low-income and middle-income countries.

Clearly, for all regions of the world, smokers who bear the full costs of their medical services will not be imposing costs on others, however much greater those costs may be than nonsmokers'. But much medical care, especially that associated with hospital treatment, is financed either through government budgets or through private insurance. To the extent that contributions to either of these financing mechanisms—in the form of taxes and insurance premiums—are not differentially higher for smokers, the higher medical costs attributable to smokers will be at least partly borne by nonsmokers.

For example, in high-income countries, public expenditure on health accounts for about 65 percent of all health expenditures, or about 6 percent of

GDP. Thus, if smokers have higher net lifetime healthcare costs, then non-smokers will subsidize the healthcare costs of smokers. The exact contribution is complex and variable, depending on the type of coverage, and the source of taxation that is used to pay for public expenditures. If, for example, only the healthcare costs of those over 65 are publicly funded, then the net use of public revenues by smokers may be small, to the extent that many require smoking-related medical care and die *before* they reach this age. Equally, if public expenditures are financed out of consumption taxes, including cigarette taxes, then smokers may not be imposing costs on others. Once again, the situation differs in low- and middle-income countries, where the public component of total healthcare expenditure is on average lower than in high-income countries, at around 44 percent of the total, or 2 percent of GDP. However, as countries spend more on health, the share of total expenditure that is met by public finance tends to rise too.

While it is thus a complex issue to assess the relative healthcare costs of smokers and nonsmokers, the issue of pensions has proved at least as contentious. Some analysts have argued that smokers in high-income countries contribute more than nonsmokers to public pension schemes, because many pay contributions until around retirement age and then die before they can claim a substantial proportion of their benefits.[1] However, a quarter of regular smokers are killed by tobacco in middle age, and may therefore die before they have paid their full pension contributions. At present, it is not known whether, overall, smokers in high-income countries do contribute more or less to public pensions than nonsmokers. However, the issue is not currently relevant to many of the low-income and middle-income countries. In low-income countries only about one in 10 adults has a public pension, and in middle-income countries the proportion is between a quarter and half of the population, depending on the income level of the individual country.

In sum, smokers clearly impose direct costs, such as health damage, on nonsmokers. There are probably also financial costs, for example in healthcare, although they are more difficult to identify or quantify.

Appropriate responses for governments

Given the three problems we identify, it appears unlikely that most smokers either know the full extent of their risks or bear all of the costs of their choice. Thus, their consumption choices may result in inefficient allocation of resources. Governments may therefore be justified in intervening to adjust the incentives to consumers so that they smoke less.

Societies may consider that the strongest reason for governments to intervene is to deter children and adolescents from smoking, given the compound problem of their inadequate access to information about tobacco, their risk of becoming addicted, and their limited ability to make sound decisions. Governments also have a justification for intervening to prevent smokers from imposing direct physical costs on nonsmokers. The justification for protecting others from smokers' financial costs is less strong, as the nature of those costs remains unclear. Finally, some societies would consider that there is a role for government in providing adults with all the information they need to make informed consumption choices.

Ideally, government interventions should address each identified problem with a specific intervention. However, this is not always possible and some interventions may have broader effects. Thus, for example, children's and adolescents' imperfect judgments about the health effects of smoking would most specifically be addressed by improving their education about those effects, and by improving their parents' education. However, in reality, children respond poorly to health education and parents are imperfect agents, not always acting in their children's best interests. In reality, taxation—albeit a blunt instrument—is the most effective and practical method of deterring children and adolescents from smoking. Evidence from a number of studies shows that children and adolescents are less likely to take up smoking, and that their smoking peers are more likely to quit, if the price of cigarettes rises.

The most specific measure to protect nonsmokers would be the imposition of restrictions on where individuals may smoke. While this would protect nonsmokers in public places, it would not reduce the substantial exposure to others' smoke in the home. Thus taxes would be an additional method of making smokers bear the costs that they impose on nonsmokers.

To address the problem of the financial costs imposed on nonsmokers, such as any excess cost of healthcare for smokers, the most direct mechanism would be to make healthcare financing systems reflect individuals' smoking behavior: thus, for example, smokers should pay higher premiums than nonsmokers, or be required to open healthcare savings accounts that reflect their likely higher costs. In practice, an easier way to make smokers contribute more would be to levy a tobacco tax.

In theory, if cigarette taxes are to be used to deter children and adolescents from smoking, then the tax on children should be higher than the tax on adults. Such differential tax treatment would, however, be virtually impossible to implement. Yet a uniform rate for children and adults, the more practical option, would impose a burden on adults. Societies may nevertheless consider that it is justifiable to impose this burden on adults in order to protect children. Moreover, if adults reduce their cigarette consumption, children may smoke less too, given evidence that children's propensity to smoke is influenced by whether their parents, and other adult role models, smoke.

One way to implement a differential tax system for children and adults would be to restrict children's access to cigarettes. In theory, such restrictions would effectively increase the price that children must pay for tobacco, without affecting the price paid by adults. In practice, however, there is little evidence that existing restrictions work in high-income countries. In low- and middle-income countries, where the capacity to administer and enforce such restrictions is likely to be less, they would be even more difficult to implement. Therefore, to deter children from smoking, the second-best instrument, higher taxes, is favored.

Dealing with addiction

In addition to the need to correct for the inefficiencies that arise from smokers' consumption choices, there is the need to address the problem of addiction. Because of addiction, adult smokers are faced with high costs if they want to reverse decisions that were largely made in youth. Societies may choose to provide interventions that would help would-be quitters to reduce these costs. These interventions include increased access to information that will alert the smoker to the costs of continuing to smoke and the benefits of quitting, and wider access to cessation therapies that would lower the costs of quitting. Clearly, increased taxation may induce some smokers to quit, but it will also impose costs on them. These costs will be the lost perceived benefits of smoking and additional physical costs associated with withdrawal from their addiction. Policymakers could reduce the costs by widening smokers' access to cessation therapies. We discuss the question of withdrawal costs further in chapter 6. For children who have not yet become addicted to nicotine, meanwhile, taxation would be an effective strategy because there would be no withdrawal costs associated with the decision not to smoke.

We turn now to consider some interventions that have already been adopted by some governments to control tobacco. Each of these interventions is evaluated in turn. In chapter 4, we discuss measures intended to reduce the demand for tobacco, and in chapter 5 we evaluate measures intended to reduce its supply.

Note

1. Even if smokers reduce the net costs imposed on others by dying young, it would be misleading to suggest that society is better off because of these premature deaths. To do so would be to accept the logic that says society is better off without its older adults.

CHAPTER 4

Measures to Reduce the Demand for Tobacco

Countries with successful tobacco control policies employ a mix of approaches. We now discuss each in turn, summarizing the evidence for their effectiveness.

Raising cigarette taxes

For centuries, tobacco has been considered an ideal consumer good for taxation: it is not a necessity, it is consumed widely, and demand for it is relatively inelastic, so it is likely to be a reliable and easily administered source of government revenue. Adam Smith, writing in *Wealth of Nations* in 1776, suggested that, through such a tax, the poor "might be relieved from some of the most burdensome taxes; from those which are imposed either upon the necessaries of life, or upon the materials of manufacture." A tobacco tax, Smith argued, would allow poor people to "live better, work cheaper, and to send their goods cheaper to market."[1] Demand for their work would increase, in turn raising the incomes of poor people and benefiting the entire economy.

Two centuries later, almost all governments tax tobacco, sometimes heavily, by a variety of different methods. Their motives have almost always been to generate revenue, but in more recent years taxes have also reflected an increasing concern with the need to minimize the health damage of smoking.

This section reviews the evidence on how increased taxation affects the demand for cigarettes and other tobacco products. It concludes that raising taxes does significantly reduce the consumption of tobacco. Importantly, the impact of higher taxes is likely to be greatest on young people, who are more responsive to price rises than older people. Equally important, the discussion concludes that higher taxes will reduce the demand for tobacco most sharply in low- and middle-income countries where smokers are more responsive to price increases than in the high-income countries. Even with this reduced demand, however, governments' revenues need not be harmed. Indeed, as we shall show in chapter 8, higher taxes may bring substantially higher revenues in the short to medium term.

Here, we briefly summarize the types of tobacco tax used by most governments and assess how price increases affect demand. The evidence from low- and middle-income countries is compared with that from high-income countries. The implications for policy are discussed.

Types of tobacco tax

Tobacco taxes can take several forms. *Specific* tobacco taxes, added as a fixed amount to the price of cigarettes, allow the greatest flexibility and allow governments to raise the tax with less risk that the industry will respond with actions that keep low the real amount charged. *Ad valorem* taxes, such as value-added taxes or sales taxes, are a percentage of the base price and are imposed by virtually all countries—often on top of the specific excise tax. *Ad valorem* taxes may be imposed at the point of sale or, as in many African countries, on the wholesale price. Taxes may vary according to the place of manufacture or the type of product; for example, some governments impose higher taxes on cigarettes produced abroad than on domestically produced ones, or on high-tar cigarettes compared with low-tar. An increasing number of countries now earmark taxes raised on tobacco for antismoking activities or other specific activities. For example, one of China's largest cities, Chongqing, and several U.S. states earmark part of the revenue from tobacco taxes for education about tobacco's effects, counter-advertising, and other control activities. Other countries use earmarked tobacco taxes to support health services.

The amount of tax charged varies from country to country (Figure 4.1). In the high-income countries, taxes amount to two-thirds or more of the retail price of a pack of cigarettes. In contrast, in the lower-income countries, taxes amount to not more than half the retail price of a pack of cigarettes.

The effect of raising taxes on cigarette consumption

A basic law of economics states that as the price of a commodity rises, the quantity demanded of that product will fall. In the past, researchers have argued that

FIGURE 4.1   AVERAGE CIGARETTE PRICE, TAX, AND PERCENTAGE OF TAX
SHARE PER PACK, BY WORLD BANK INCOME GROUPS, 1996

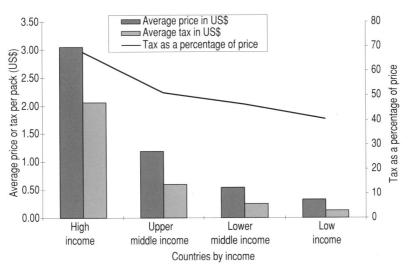

Source: Authors' calculations.

tobacco's addictive nature would make it an exception to this rule: smokers, according to this argument, are sufficiently addicted to smoking that they will pay any price and continue to smoke the same number of cigarettes to satisfy their needs. However, a growing volume of research now shows that this argument is wrong and that smokers' demand for tobacco, while inelastic, is nevertheless strongly affected by its price. For example, tax increases in Canada between 1982 and 1992 led to a steep increase in the real price of cigarettes, and consumption fell substantially (Figure 4.2a). Similar decreases in cigarette consumption as the result of tax increases have been seen in the United Kingdom and a number of other countries. Conversely, lower taxes increased cigarette consumption in South Africa between 1979 and 1989 (Figure 4.2b). Researchers have consistently found that price increases encourage some people to stop smoking, that they prevent others from starting in the first place, and that they reduce the number of ex-smokers who resume the habit.

How addiction affects the response to higher prices

Models that attempt to assess the impact of nicotine addiction on the effects of

FIGURE 4.2   CIGARETTE PRICE AND CONSUMPTION GO IN OPPOSITE TRENDS
4.2a   *Real price of cigarettes and annual cigarette consumption per capita, Canada,*
1989–1995

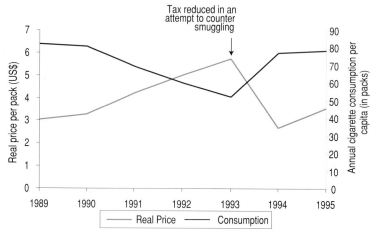

4.2b   *Real price of cigarettes and annual cigarette consumption per adult (15 years of*
age and above), South Africa, 1970–1989

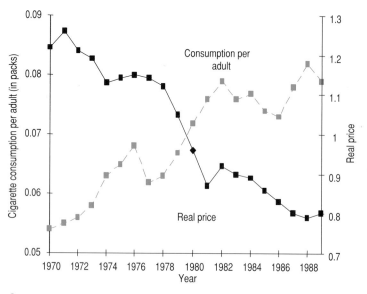

Note: Consumption is derived from sales data.
Sources: 4.2a: Authors' calculations.   4.2b: Saloojee, Yussuf. 1995. "Price and Income
Elasticity of Demand for Cigarettes in South Africa." In Slama, K. ed., *Tobacco and Health*.
New York, NY: Plenum Press; and Townsend, Joy. 1998. "The Role of Taxation Policy in
Tobacco Control." In Abedian, I., and others, eds. *The Economics of Tobacco Control*.
Cape Town, South Africa: Applied Fiscal Research Centre, University of Cape Town.

price increases make varying assumptions about whether smokers look ahead at the consequences of their actions or not. However, all models agree that, for an addictive substance such as nicotine, an individual's current consumption levels will be determined by his or her past consumption levels as well as by the current price of the good. This relationship between past consumption and current consumption has important implications for modeling the impact of price rises on demand for tobacco. If smokers are addicted, they will respond relatively slowly to price increases, but their response will be greater in the long term. The economics literature suggests that a real and permanent price increase will have approximately twice as great an impact on demand in the long run as in the short run.

Differing responses to price increases in low-income and high-income countries

When the price of a good rises, people on low incomes are in general more likely to cut back their consumption of that good than people on high incomes; and, conversely, when the price falls, they are more likely to increase their consumption. The extent to which consumers' demand for a good changes in response to a price change is known as the price elasticity of demand. For example, if a price rise of 10 percent causes the quantity demanded to fall by 5 percent, the elasticity of demand is -0.5. The more price-responsive consumers are, the greater is the elasticity of demand.

Estimates of elasticity vary from study to study, but there is reasonable evidence that in middle-income and low-income countries, elasticity of demand is greater than in high-income countries. In the United States, for example, researchers have found that a price rise of 10 percent for a pack of cigarettes decreases demand by about 4 percent (an elasticity of -0.4). Studies in China have concluded that a price rise of 10 percent reduces demand by more than in high-income countries; depending on the study, the elasticity estimates range between about -0.6 and -1.0. Studies in Brazil and South Africa have produced results in the same range. For low- and middle-income countries as a whole, then, a reasonable estimate of the average elasticity of demand would be -0.8, based on current data.

There are further reasons why people in low-income countries are more likely to respond to cigarette price rises than people in high-income countries. The age structure of most low-income countries' populations is generally younger and research from the high-income countries suggests that, on the whole, young people are more price-responsive than older people. This is partly because they have lower disposable incomes, partly because some may, as yet, be less heavily addicted to nicotine, partly because of their more present-oriented behavior, and partly because they are more susceptible to peer influences. Thus, if one young person stops smoking because he or she can no longer afford to do it, friends are more likely to follow suit than amongst older age groups. A study by the U.S. Centers for Disease Control and Prevention found that demand elasticity among young adults aged between 18 and 24 in the United States was -0.6, higher than for smokers overall. Researchers conclude that when prices are high, not only are existing young smokers more likely to quit, but that fewer potential young smokers will take up the habit.

Based on the evidence currently available, we can therefore draw two clear conclusions. First, that tax increases are a highly effective way to reduce tobacco consumption in low- and middle-income countries, where most smokers now live; and, second, that the effect of such tax increases will be more marked in these countries than in high-income countries.

The potential impact of tax increases on global demand for tobacco

For the purposes of this report, researchers have modeled the potential impact of a range of tax increases on demand for cigarettes worldwide. The design of the model and its inputs are described in Box 4.1. The assumptions on which the model is based, concerning price elasticity, health impact, and other variables, are highly conservative. Thus the results are likely to be underestimates of the potential. The model reveals that even modest price increases could have a striking impact on the prevalence of smoking and on the number of tobacco-related premature deaths among those alive in 1995. The researchers calculate that if there were a sustained real rise in the price of cigarettes of 10 percent over the average estimated price in each region, 40 million people worldwide would quit smoking, and many more who would otherwise have taken up smoking would be deterred from doing so. Given that not all quitters would avoid death, the number of premature deaths avoided is still extraordinary by any standards—10 million, or 3 percent of all tobacco-related deaths—from this price increase alone. Nine million of the premature deaths avoided would be in developing countries, of which 4 million would be in East Asia and the Pacific (Table 4.1).

Difficulties in computing an optimal tax level for cigarettes

There have been various attempts to decide what the "right" level of tax on cigarettes should be. To decide that level, the policymaker needs to have certain empirical facts, some of which may not yet be available, such as the scale of the costs to nonsmokers. The level also depends on incomes and assumptions on the basis of values that differ from one society to another. For example, some societies would place greater importance on the need to protect children than others.

TABLE 4.1   POTENTIAL NUMBER OF SMOKERS PERSUADED TO QUIT, AND
LIVES SAVED, BY A PRICE INCREASE OF 10 PERCENT
Impact on smokers alive in 1995, by World Bank region
(millions)

Region	Change in number of smokers	Change in number of deaths
East Asia and Pacific	−16	−4
Eastern Europe and Central Asia	−6	−1.5
Latin America and the Caribbean	−4	−1.0
Middle East and North Africa	−2	−0.4
South Asia (cigarettes)	−3	−0.7
South Asia (*bidis*)	−2	−0.4
Sub-Saharan Africa	−3	−0.7
Low/Middle Income	−36	−9
High Income	−4	−1
World	−40	−10

Note: Numbers have been rounded.
Source: Ranson, Kent, P. Jha, F. Chaloupka, and A Yurekli. *Effectiveness and Cost-effectiveness of Price Increases and Other Tobacco Control Policy Interventions.* Background paper.

BOX 4.1 ESTIMATING THE IMPACT OF CONTROL MEASURES ON GLOBAL TOBACCO
CONSUMPTION: THE INPUTS TO THE MODEL

First, the researchers took estimates of the population in each region, with breakdown by age groups and gender, using standard World Bank population projections for the seven World Bank regions (see Appendix D). Second, they estimated the prevalence of smoking, by gender, for each of the seven regions, using a compiled set of more than 80 studies from individual countries used by the World Health Organization (the data are shown in chapter 1, Table 1.1). In the case of India, where *bidis* are a widespread alternative to cigarettes, the prevalence of both types of smoking was derived from local studies. Third, using the available data, the team estimated the age profile of smokers in each region, extrapolating from large-scale individual country studies, and estimated the ratio of adult smokers to youth smokers. Fourth, the total number of smokers and the predicted number of deaths attributable to tobacco were estimated by region, gender, and age. In this step, the researchers assumed that only one in three smokers in developed countries eventually die of their habit. This assumption is conservative, given studies from the United Kingdom, the United States, and elsewhere suggesting that the actual figure is one in two, and is likely to be an under-

(continued on next page)

BOX 4.1 (CONTINUED)

estimate, as recent research from China indicates that the proportion of smokers killed by tobacco will soon equal that found in the West.

Next, the researchers estimated the number of cigarettes or *bidis* smoked each day by each smoker in every region, using WHO figures and various published epidemiological studies. They also made estimates of the number smoked by adults and by youths in each region to arrive at a ratio of adult-to-youth daily smoking rate.

The researchers then attempted to gauge the price elasticity of demand for cigarettes in each region, using data from more than 60 studies. Where more than one study had been done in any given country the resulting figures were averaged. The researchers combined the figures to arrive at averages for low- and high-income regions. These figures were also weighted by age, since young people are more price-responsive than older people. The short-run price elasticity for high-income countries was calculated to be relatively low, that is -0.4, whereas for low-income countries it was calculated to be -0.8.

The researchers assumed that, in line with one major study, half of the effect of a price increase would be on the number of people who smoke, and half would be on the number of cigarettes smoked by those who continued. Also in line with other research evidence, they assumed that younger quitters would be more likely to avoid tobacco-related deaths than older quitters, and that the risks of tobacco-related death would persist for all continuing smokers, despite a reduction in the number of cigarettes smoked.

All of the variables in the model were subjected to a sensitivity analysis to allow for uncertainty, with ranges of 75 percent to 125 percent of the baseline values used in the calculations. It should be stressed that the assumptions on which the model has been based are all conservative ones, so that the results are likely to err on the low rather than the high side.

In economic terms the optimal tax would be one that equates the marginal social cost of the last cigarette consumed with its marginal social benefits. However, as we saw in the previous chapter, the magnitude of those social costs and benefits is unknown, nearly impossible to measure, and the subject of considerable ongoing controversy. Few doubt that smokers impose physical costs on nonsmokers who are obliged to inhale their smoke, with the biggest burden of passive smoking borne by the children and spouses of smokers. Yet, since some economists consider the family to be the basic decisionmaking unit in society, they regard spouses' and children's exposure to tobacco smoke as an internal cost that is taken into account in the family's decisions about smoking, rather than an external cost imposed by smokers on others. Meanwhile, the scale of other costs, such as those from publicly financed healthcare for treating smoking-related diseases, is difficult to judge, as we have seen. Studies from the United States that attempt to compute the economically optimal tax produce a wide range of estimates, from a few cents to several dollars.

Another approach to setting tax levels is to select a rate that would achieve a specific reduction in cigarette consumption and hence meet a specific public health target, rather than one that will cover the social costs of smoking. Yet another objective would be to set tax levels to maximize the revenues generated from these relatively efficient taxes.

Rather than attempt to suggest an optimal tax level, this report proposes a more pragmatic approach: to observe the tax levels adopted by countries with comprehensive and effective tobacco control policies. In such countries, the tax component of the price of a pack of cigarettes is between two-thirds and four-fifths of the total retail cost. These levels can be used as a yardstick for proportionate increases in prices elsewhere.[2]

Nonprice measures to reduce demand: consumer information, bans on advertising and promotion, and smoking restrictions

There is extensive evidence from the high-income countries that the provision of information to adult consumers about the addictive nature of tobacco and its burden of fatal and disabling diseases can help to reduce their consumption of cigarettes. In this section, we review what is known about the effectiveness of a range of types of such information, including publicized research into the health consequences of smoking; warnings on cigarette packs and on advertisements; and counter-advertising. We shall also summarize what is known about the effects of the tobacco advertising and promotion activities, and what happens when these activities are banned. Because the different types of information are often available to consumers concurrently, it is difficult to disaggregate their individual effects, but the growing body of research and experience in high-income countries suggests that each can have a significant impact. Importantly, the impact appears to vary across different social groups. In general, young people appear to be less responsive to information about the health effects of tobacco than older adults, and more educated people respond more quickly to new information than those with no or minimal education. An awareness of these differences is useful for policymakers when planning a mix of interventions that is tailored to the particular needs of their own country.

Publicized findings of research on the health effects of smoking

The long-term downward trend in smoking prevalence in most high-income countries over the past three decades has coincided with a long-term upward trend in people's levels of knowledge about the harmful effects of smoking. In 1950, in the United States, only 45 percent of adults identified smoking as a cause of lung cancer. By 1990, 95 percent did so. Over approximately the same period, the proportion of the U.S. population that smoked fell from more than 40 percent to about 25 percent.

On many occasions in the high-income countries, the public has been exposed to "information shocks" about the health effects of smoking, such as the publication of official reports on the subject that receive wide media coverage. The impact of these has been studied in such diverse countries as Finland, Greece, Switzerland, Turkey, the United Kingdom, the United States, and South Africa. In general, the impact is greatest, and most sustained, at a relatively early stage in a population's epidemic of tobacco-related disease, when general awareness of the health risks of smoking are low. As knowledge increases, new information shocks become less effective.

An analysis in the United States, based on times-series data between the 1930s and the late 1970s, suggests that three information shocks, including an influential report of the Surgeon General in 1964, together reduced consumption by as much as 30 percent over the period. In more recent decades, studies from several high-income countries have concluded that publicized information about the health effects of tobacco has been responsible for a sustained decline in consumption. For example, between 1960 and 1994 in the United States, parents decreased their consumption of cigarettes much more rapidly than single adults living without children. Researchers have concluded that parents' increasing awareness of the hazards of passive smoking for their children has deterred them from smoking.

In low-income and middle-income countries to date, there has been little research to monitor the impact of information shocks. However, smoking trends in China are being monitored following the recent publication of major studies of the health effects of smoking there. Clearly, a prerequisite for publicizing data that portray the health consequences of smoking is to collect those data in the first place. Recent moves in South Africa and India to "count the tobacco dead" through the inexpensive method of noting individuals' smoking status on their death certificates should help to provide data that are needed to describe the shape and size of the tobacco epidemic in each region.

Warning labels

Even in countries where consumers have had reasonable access to information about the health effects of smoking, the evidence suggests that there are widespread misperceptions about these effects, due, in part, to cigarette packaging and labeling. For example, in the past two decades, many manufacturers have labeled certain classes of cigarette as "low tar" and "low nicotine." Many smokers in high-income countries believe that these brands are safer than other cigarettes, although the research literature concludes that no cigarettes are safe. Studies suggest that many consumers are confused about the constituents of tobacco smoke, and that packaging fails to give them adequate information about the products they are buying.

Since the early 1960s a growing number of governments have required cigarette manufacturers to print health warnings on their products. By 1991, 77 countries required such warnings, although very few of these countries insisted on strong warnings with rotating messages, such as the one illustrated in Figure 4.3.

A study from Turkey suggests that health warnings caused consumption there to fall by about 8 percent over six years. In South Africa, when serious warning labels were introduced in 1994, there was a significant fall in consumption. More than half (58 percent) of smokers questioned for that study said they were motivated by the warning labels to quit or reduce their smoking. However, one key weakness of warning labels is that they will not reach some poorer individuals, particularly children and adolescents, in low-income countries. Among such consumers, it is common to buy cigarettes singly rather than in packs.

It has sometimes been argued that, in the more informed populations where smoking has been widespread for many decades, smoking prevalence is unlikely to fall much lower than it has already as a result of cigarette pack warning labels. However, evidence from Australia, Canada, and Poland suggests that such labels can still be effective, provided that they are large, prominent, and contain hard-hitting and specific factual information. In Poland in the late 1990s, new warning labels that occupy 30 percent of each of the two largest sides on the cigarette pack have been found to be strongly linked with smokers' decisions to quit or cut down their smoking. Among Polish male smokers, 3 percent said they had quit following the introduction of the labels; an additional 16 percent said they had tried quitting, and a further 14 percent said they understood the health effects of smoking better because of the warnings. Among women, the effects were similar. In Australia, warning labels were strengthened in 1995. The impact appears to have been greater in inducing smokers to quit than when the older, less strongly worded labels were used. In Canada, a survey

FIGURE 4.3   A STRONG WARNING LABEL
Proposed prototype of plain packaging for cigarettes in Australia

Source: Institute of Medicine. *Growing Up Tobacco Free: Preventing Nicotine Addiction in Children and Youths.* 1994. National Academy Press. Washington, D.C.

in 1996 suggested that half of smokers intending to quit or cut back their consumption were motivated by what they had read on their cigarette packs.

Mass media counter-advertising

There have been a number of studies to analyze the impact of negative messages about smoking on cigarette consumption. These negative messages, or counter-advertising, are disseminated by governments and health-promotion agencies, and they have been consistently found to reduce overall consumption, according to studies at both national and local levels from North America, Australia, Europe, and Israel. Swiss researchers concluded from a study of adult tobacco consumption conducted between 1954 and 1981 that antismoking publicity in the mass media permanently reduced consumption by 11 percent over the period. In Finland and Turkey, anti-smoking campaigns are also judged to have contributed to declines in consumption.

School antismoking educational programs

School antismoking programs are widespread, particularly in the high-income countries. However, they appear to be less effective than many other types of information dissemination. Even programs that have initially reduced the up-take of smoking appear to have only a temporary effect; they can somewhat delay the initiation of smoking but not prevent it. The apparent weakness of school-based programs may have less to do with their nature than with the audience at which they are targeted. As we have seen, adolescent responses to information about the long-term consequences of an action on their health are not the same as adult responses, partly because of more present-oriented be-havior and partly because adolescents tend to rebel against adults' advice.

Cigarette advertising and promotion

Policymakers who are interested in controlling tobacco need to know whether cigarette advertising and promotion affect consumption. The answer is that they almost certainly do, although the data are not straightforward. The key conclusion is that bans on advertising and promotion prove effective, but only if they are comprehensive, covering all media and all uses of brand names and logos. We discuss the evidence briefly here.

There is a vigorous debate about the impact of cigarette advertising on consumers. On the one hand, public health advocates argue that such advertis-ing does increase consumption. In contrast, the tobacco industry has argued that its advertising does not recruit new smokers but merely encourages con-firmed smokers to stay with, or switch to, a particular brand. On the face of it, empirical studies of the relationship between advertising and sales have tended to conclude either that advertising has no positive effect on consumption, or that it shows only a very modest positive effect. However, these studies may be misleading, for the following reasons. First, economic theory suggests that ad-vertising will have a diminishing marginal impact on demand; that is, when advertising for a product increases, consumers will gradually respond less and less to additional advertising, and, ultimately, increased advertising will stop making any impact on them at all. Advertising in the tobacco industry is at a relatively high level, around 6 percent of sales revenues, about 50 percent higher than the average industry. Thus, any increased consumption that may result from increased advertising is likely to be very small and difficult to detect. This does not mean that, in the absence of advertising, consumption would necessar-ily be as high as it is in the presence of advertising—only that the marginal impact of an increase in advertising is negligible. Second, data that record the impact of advertising on sales are usually highly aggregated for relatively long time periods, for all advertisers, in all media, and often over large populations.

Any subtle changes that might be apparent at a more disaggregated level of analysis are therefore obscured. In studies that use less aggregated data, researchers find more evidence of a positive effect of advertising on consumption, but such studies are expensive and time-consuming and, therefore, rare.

Given the problems with these approaches, researchers have turned instead to studying what happens when tobacco advertising and promotion are banned as an indirect means of gauging their effect on consumption.

The impact of advertising bans

When governments ban tobacco advertising in one medium, such as television, the industry can substitute advertising in other media with little or no effect on overall marketing expenditures. Accordingly, studies that have examined the effect of partial cigarette advertising bans have found little or no effect on smoking. However, where there are multiple restrictions on advertising in all media and on promotional activities, there are relatively few alternative outlets for the industry. Since 1972, most high-income countries have introduced stronger restrictions across more media and on various forms of sponsorship. A recent study of 22 high-income countries based on data from 1970 to 1992 concluded that comprehensive bans on cigarette advertising and promotion can reduce smoking, but more limited partial bans have little or no effect. If the most comprehensive restrictions were in place, the study concluded, tobacco consumption would fall by more than 6 percent in high-income countries. Modeling based on these estimates suggests that the European Union's ban on advertising (see Box 4.2) could reduce cigarette consumption within the European Union by nearly 7 percent. Another study of 100 countries compared consumption trends over time in those with relatively complete bans on advertising and promotion and those with no such bans. In the countries with nearly complete bans, the downward trend in consumption was much steeper (Figure 4.4). It is important to note that, in this study, other factors may also have contributed to the decline in consumption in some countries.

Beyond the economic literature, meanwhile, there are other types of research, such as surveys of children's recall of advertising messages, that conclude that advertising and promotion do indeed affect demand for cigarettes and attract new recruits. Children's attention is attracted by such advertising, and they remember its messages. There is also growing evidence that the industry is directing increasing shares of its advertising and promotion activity toward markets where there is judged to be growth or potential for growth, including some youth markets and specific minority groups among whom smoking has until recently been uncommon. This noneconomic body of research may be of particular interest to policymakers concerned about smoking trends within specific groups in the population.

FIGURE 4.4   COMPREHENSIVE ADVERTISING BANS REDUCE CIGARETTE
CONSUMPTION
*Trends in weighted cigarette consumption per capita in countries with a comprehensive
ban compared with countries with no ban*

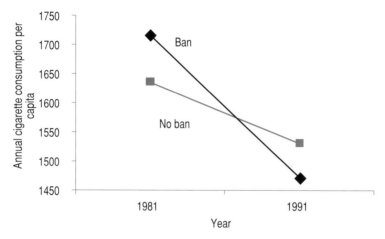

Note: The analysis covers 102 countries, with or without a comprehensive ban on tobacco
advertising, in relation to changes in cigarette comsumption data per adult aged 15 to 64,
weighted by population, between 1980–82 and 1990–92. Countries with comprehensive
bans start at a higher consumption level than the nonban group, but end the period with a
lower consumption rate. The change is due to a higher rate of decrease in consumption
for the ban group than the nonban group.
Source: Saffer, Henry. *The Control of Tobacco Advertising and Promotion.* Background
paper.

Restrictions on smoking in public and workplaces

A growing number of countries and states are now implementing restrictions
on smoking in public places such as restaurants and transport facilities. In
some countries, such as the United States, some workplaces are also covered
by public restrictions. The most obvious benefit of these restrictions is clearly
to nonsmokers, who are spared exposure to the health risks and nuisance of
environmental tobacco smoke. But, as we have seen, most nonsmokers' exposure to others' smoke is not in public places or workplaces, but in the home.
These restrictions therefore represent only a partial means of addressing the
needs of nonsmokers.

   A second effect of smoking restrictions is that they reduce some smokers'
consumption of cigarettes and induce some to quit. In the United States, such

In 1989, as part of a wider initiative against cancer, the European Commission proposed a directive to restrict the advertising of tobacco products in the press and by means of billboards and posters. The European Parliament amended the Commission's proposal in 1990 and voted for an advertising ban.

The Commission observed that it could only secure agreement for a partial ban at the time, but added that a new proposal for a total ban might be made, depending on progress achieved by individual member states. In June 1991 the Commission introduced a modified proposal for a directive on tobacco.

In the period between 1992 and 1996 no progress was made in implementing the proposal because of opposition from at least three member states, Germany, the Netherlands, and the United Kingdom. However, opposition in the United Kingdom collapsed in 1997, when the Labour Party won the general election, with a manifesto commitment to introduce a tobacco advertising ban. The text of the proposed directive was finally adopted by the Commission in June 1998. The directive stipulates that all direct and indirect advertising (including sponsorship) of tobacco products will be banned within the European Union, with full and final enforcement of all provisions by October 2006. Its key points are as follows:

- All member states of the European Union must introduce national legislation not later than 30 July 2001.
- All advertisements in the print media must cease within one further year.
- Sponsorship (with the exception of events or activities organized at a global level) must cease within two further years.
- Tobacco sponsorship of world events, such as Formula One motor racing, may continue for a further three years, but must end by 1 October 2006. During this period of phaseout, there must be a reduction in overall sponsorship support as well as voluntary restraint on tobacco publicity surrounding these events.
- Product information is allowed at points of sale.
- Tobacco trade publications may carry tobacco advertising.
- Third-country publications, not intended specifically for the European Union market, are not affected by the ban.

This directive is now under implementation.

restrictions have reduced tobacco consumption by between 4 and 10 percent, according to various estimates. For such restrictions to work, it appears that there must be a general level of social support for them, and an awareness of the health consequences of exposure to environmental tobacco smoke. Outside the United States, there are comparatively few data on the effectiveness of indoor smoking restrictions.

The potential impact of nonprice measures on global demand for tobacco

We have described the evidence for the effectiveness of a number of nonprice measures, including information for consumers, dissemination of scientific reports and research, warning labels, counter-advertising, comprehensive bans on advertising and promotion, and smoking restrictions. As part of the background work for this report, the model described in Box 4.1 was used to assess the potential impact of a comprehensive package of these nonprice measures on cigarette consumption worldwide. Because until now there have been few attempts to estimate the aggregate impact of these measures, the model was constructed on conservative assumptions. It assumes, on the basis of the existing measures of effectiveness for individual nonprice measures, that their combined impact would be to persuade between 2 and 10 percent of consumers to quit. To be conservative, the model assumes that the measures would have no impact on the numbers of cigarettes smoked daily by those who do not stop.

Based on these assumptions, a package of nonprice measures could reduce the number of smokers alive in 1995 by 23 million worldwide, even at the lower end of the estimate—that is, if packages implemented worldwide reduced the number of consumers by only 2 percent (see Table 4.2). Using the previous assumptions about the number of quitters who would avoid death, the model suggests that 5 million lives could be saved.

Nicotine replacement therapy and other cessation interventions

In addition to higher taxes and nonprice measures, there is a third set of measures to help reduce tobacco consumption. These are cessation treatments and programs of various types, including individual training, hospital treatment, counseling programs, and the growing range of pharmacological products designed to aid cessation, such as nicotine replacement therapy (NRT) products and an antidepressant drug with the generic name bupropion. NRT products, in the form of patches, gums, sprays, and inhalators deliver low doses of nicotine without delivering the other harmful constituents of tobacco smoke. Used properly, NRT is regarded as safe and effective by major medical organizations in the high-income countries. A large body of research concludes that it

TABLE 4.2: POTENTIAL NUMBER OF SMOKERS PERSUADED TO QUIT, AND
LIVES SAVED, BY A PACKAGE OF NONPRICE MEASURES
(Millions)
For smokers alive in 1995

Region	Change in number of smokers if package reduces the prevalence of smoking by:		Change in number of deaths if package reduces the prevalence of smoking by:	
	2 percent	10 percent	2 percent	10 percent
East Asia and Pacific	–8	–40	–2	–10
Eastern Europe and Central Asia	–3	–15	–0.7	–3
Latin America and Caribbean	–2	–10	–0.5	–2
Middle East and North Africa	–0.8	–4	–0.2	–1
South Asia (cigarettes)	–2	–9	–0.3	–2
South Asia (*bidis*)	–2	–10	–0.4	–2
Sub-Saharan Africa	–1	–7	–0.4	–2
Low/Middle Income	–19	–93	–4	–22
High Income	–4	–21	–1	–5
World	–23	–114	–5	–27

Note: Numbers have been rounded.
Source: Ranson, Kent, P. Jha, F. Chaloupka, and A. Yurekli. *Effectiveness and Cost-effectiveness of Price Increases and Other Tobacco Control Policy Interventions.* Background paper.

doubles the success rates of other cessation efforts, whether or not other interventions are used in parallel (Table 4.3). Bupropion has also been shown to be
effective in trials in the United States. A key advantage of NRT is that it can be
self-administered. This enhances its practical potential to smokers who wish
to quit in countries where there are limited resources for intensive support by
health professionals.

NRT is prescribed solely for treating the symptoms of nicotine withdrawal
in smokers who are trying to quit. NRT products have not, to date, been linked
with any cardiovascular or respiratory disease, and there is consensus that they
are a much safer source of nicotine than tobacco. Nicotine does, of course,
produce physiological effects, including raising blood pressure. However, compared with cigarettes, the doses of nicotine delivered by NRT products are
smaller, and they are delivered more slowly. NRT represents a means of reducing the costs of quitting in regular smokers.

The availability of NRT varies from country to country. In some high-
income countries, products are sold over the counter, while in others they are
available only through prescription. Models based on data from the United
States suggest that, if NRT were made available over the counter, significantly

TABLE 4.3 EFFECTIVENESS OF VARIOUS CESSATION APPROACHES

Intervention and comparison	Increase in percentage of smokers abstaining for 6 months or more
Brief advice to stop (3 to 10 minutes) by clinician versus no advice	2 to 3
Adding NRT to brief advice versus brief advice alone or brief advice plus placebo	6
Intensive support (for example, smokers' clinic) plus NRT versus intensive support or intensive support plus placebo	8

Source: Raw, Martin, and others. 1999. Data are from the Agency for Health Care Policy and Research, and the Cochrane Library.

more people would quit and more lives would be saved than if NRT were available only through prescription. Over five years, the model predicts, almost 3,000 lives would be saved in the United States alone. There is also evidence that smokers want this type of help: in the United States, sales of NRT products increased by 150 percent between 1996, when products were first sold over the counter, and 1998.

Outside the high-income countries, the availability of NRT in any form is patchy; for example, NRT products are sold in Argentina, Brazil, Indonesia, Malaysia, Mexico, the Philippines, South Africa, and Thailand, but in some of these countries supplies are restricted to a few major urban areas. In some middle-income countries and many low-income countries, NRT products are not available at all. A day's supply of NRT products costs about the same as the average daily dose of tobacco, but because they are usually sold as a whole course, they require a comparatively large single payment. Compared with cigarettes, the sale of NRT products is highly regulated.

Given the evidence, many policymakers might consider widening access to NRT as a valuable component of tobacco control policies. One option would be to reduce the regulation on sales of these products, for example, by increasing the range of outlets and the hours of sale of such products, and reducing restrictions on packaging.

Another option, given the evidence that NRT would help to reduce the costs of quitting, would be to consider making NRT available at subsidized prices, or free, for limited periods to smokers on low incomes who wish to quit. This approach is already being tested in some settings. In the United Kingdom, for example, there are proposals for the poorest smokers to be made eligible for limited free supply of NRT if they decide to quit. Targeting such services to the poor is a challenge in all countries.

Clearly, any decision to widen access to NRT must be considered carefully. Most societies would wish to avoid promoting the sale of any addictive good to children. However, the consensus of health professionals in high-income countries is that NRT, used effectively, is beneficial and should be encouraged for adult smokers who want to quit. The cost-effectiveness of nicotine replacement therapy has not been studied widely, especially in the low-income and middle-income countries where most smokers live. It is clear that more information on cost-effectiveness would be useful for policymakers at local levels, both in determining whether these devices should have a claim on limited public funds, and in giving policymakers a firmer basis on which to act.

As background work to this report, the potential impact of more widely available NRT was modeled using the same methods as above. To be conservative, it was assumed that the effectiveness of the therapy might be lower than the available studies from high-income countries suggest. With the conservative assumption that quit rates among users of NRTs would be double that of nonusers, but that only about 6 percent of smokers would use NRTs to quit, we estimate that the 6 million smokers alive in 1995 could be enabled to quit, and 1 million deaths could be averted. If, on the other hand, 25 percent of smokers used NRT, we find that 29 million smokers alive in 1995 would be enabled to quit, and 7 million deaths could be averted.

Notes

1. Smith, Adam. *Wealth of Nations*. 1776. Version edited by Edwin Canaan, 1976. University of Chicago Press, Chicago.
2. For example, if tax is to account for four-fifths of the retail price, this requires prices to be increased by four times the manufacturer's (untaxed) price per pack. Thus, for instance, if a nontax price is equal to $0.50, then the tax rate would be 0.5 × 4 = $2. Retail price would be equal to $2 (tax) + $0.50 (manufacturing price) = $2.50. The impact on retail price would, of course, vary between countries, depending on retail factors such as the wholesale price, but broadly, an increase of this order would raise the population-weighted price by between 80 and 100 percent in low- and middle-income countries.

CHAPTER 5

Measures to Reduce the Supply of Tobacco

W HEREAS there is abundant evidence that the demand for tobacco can be reduced, there is much less evidence of success in reducing its supply. Here, we briefly discuss the experience of countries in attempting to restrict access to tobacco and to reduce its supply through trade restrictions or agricultural policies. In the second section of the chapter, we discuss one key way in which governments *can* reduce tobacco supplies, by controlling smuggling.

The limited effectiveness of most supply-side interventions

A basic observation in markets is that, if one supplier of a commodity is prevented from operating, another will quickly emerge to take its place as long as there is a strong incentive to do so. There are currently clear incentives to supply tobacco, as the discussion here sets out.

Prohibition of tobacco

Given tobacco's unprecedented capacity to damage health, a few public health advocates have called for it to be prohibited, arguing that the problem of tobacco is not in its consumption, but its production. Advocates of tobacco prohibition point to the marked reduction in alcohol-related diseases when alcohol supply was restricted earlier in the 20th century. For example, when alcohol supplies were restricted in Paris, France, during World War II, alcohol consumption fell by 80 percent per capita. Deaths from liver disease in men were halved within one year and fell by four-fifths after five years. After the war ended and alcohol became freely available, mortality from liver disease returned to prewar levels.

However, for a number of reasons the prohibition of tobacco is unlikely to be either feasible or effective. First, even when substances are prohibited, they continue to be widely used, as is the case with many illicit drugs. Second, prohibition creates its own sets of problems: it is likely to increase criminal activity and entail costly police enforcement. Third, from an economic perspective, optimal tobacco consumption is not zero. Fourth, the prohibition of tobacco is unlikely to be politically acceptable in most countries. In India, recent attempts to ban a chewed type of tobacco known as *gutka* failed, largely due to a political backlash against prohibition.

Restrictions on youth access to tobacco

There have been a number of attempts to impose restrictions on the sale of cigarettes to teenagers in high-income countries. In their existing form, such restrictions have not been shown to be successful. In general, youth restrictions are difficult to enforce, especially given that young teenagers often obtain cigarettes from their older peers, and, sometimes, from their parents. Moreover, in low-income countries where tobacco consumption is rising, the necessary systems, infrastructure, and resources for implementing such restrictions and enforcing them are much less widely available than in the high-income countries.

Crop substitution and diversification

More than 100 countries grow tobacco, of which about 80 are developing countries. Four countries account for two-thirds of the total production: in 1997, China was responsible for 42 percent of all tobacco grown, with the United States, India, and Brazil producing about 24 percent between them. The top 20 countries produce more than 90 percent of the total (see Table 5.1). Over the past two decades, the share of global production by high-income countries has fallen from 30 to 15 percent, while that by countries in the Middle East and Asia has risen from 40 to 60 percent. Africa's share rose from 4 to 6 percent, and other regions have changed little.

Whereas China uses most of its tobacco crop for its domestic market, other major producers export large proportions of theirs. Brazil, Turkey, Zimbabwe, Malawi, Greece, and Italy all export more than seven-tenths of their crop. Only two countries worldwide are significantly dependent on raw tobacco for their export earnings—Zimbabwe, with 23 percent of export earnings, and Malawi, with 61 percent. A few other countries—Bulgaria, Moldova, the Dominican

TABLE 5.1 THE TOP 30 RAW-TOBACCO-PRODUCING COUNTRIES
1997 data, ranked by production

Country	Production (1,000 metric tons)	Production change over 1994 values	Share of world total (percent)	Area (1,000 hectares)	Share of world total (percent)	Export ratio[a] (percent)	Import ratio[b] (percent)	Tobacco export revenue (as a percentage of total exports 1995)
China	3,390.0	51.5	42.12	1,880.0	38.4	2.9	4.7	0.68
United States	746.4	4.0	9.27	328.4	6.7	35.5	7.4	0.55
India	623.7	18.1	7.75	420.2	8.6	23.2	c	0.44
Brazil	576.6	30.5	7.16	329.5	6.7	77.0	0.2	2.55
Turkey	296.0	57.7	3.68	323.0	6.6	89.3	0.5	1.17
Zimbabwe	192.1	8.0	2.39	99.3	2.0	109.7	c	23.05
Indonesia	184.3	15.2	2.29	217.5	4.4	10.2	27.6	0.42
Malawi	158.6	61.7	1.97	122.3	2.5	74.2	c	60.64
Greece	132.5	-2.2	1.65	67.3	1.4	74.5	12.8	2.05
Italy	131.4	0.3	1.63	47.5	1.0	78.7	18.3	0.04
Argentina	123.2	50.3	1.53	71.0	1.5	60.6	5.1	0.59
Pakistan	86.3	-14.0	1.07	45.9	0.9	1.6	c	0.08
Bulgaria	78.2	124.3	0.97	48.5	1.0	53.5	58.3	5.40
Canada	71.1	-0.5	0.88	28.5	0.6	24.0	12.6	0.04
Thailand	69.3	17.4	0.86	47.0	1.0	48.5	15.3	0.11
Japan	68.5	-13.8	0.85	25.6	0.5	0.5	145.4	0.04
Philippines	60.9	8.7	0.76	29.4	0.6	17.2	18.3	0.17
South Korea	54.4	-44.8	0.68	27.2	0.6	8.4	26.2	0.02
Mexico	44.3	-35.1	0.55	25.4	0.5	31.8	8.3	0.11
Bangladesh	44.0	-26.7	0.55	50.3	1.0	c	16.1	0.03
Spain	42.3	0.1	0.53	13.3	0.3	53.9	126.7	0.06

(continues on next page)

TABLE 5.1 *(continued)*

Country	Production (1,000 metric tons)	Production change over 1994 values	Share of world total (percent)	Area (1,000 hectares)	Share of world total (percent)	Export ratio[a] (percent)	Import ratio[b] (percent)	Tobacco export revenue (as a percentage of total exports) 1995
Poland	41.7	−3.3	0.52	19.0	0.4	6.9	66.4	0.12
Cuba	37.0	117.6	0.46	59.0	1.2	13.5	0.8	n.a.
Moldova	35.8	−15.8	0.45	17.2	0.4	61.4	6.7	6.90
Vietnam	32.0	N/A	0.40	36.0	0.7	n.a.	n.a.	0.04
Dominican Republic	30.3	41.7	0.38	21.2	0.4	58.1	2.2	5.26
Macedonia	30.0	n.a.	0.37	22.0	0.4	n.a.	n.a.	5.44
Kyrgyzstan	30.0	−33.3	0.37	12.0	0.2	76.7	3.3	6.96
South Africa	29.0	−1.4	0.34	14.9	0.3	41.5	55.5	0.31
Tanzania	25.1	15.1	0.31	n.a.	n.a.	55.8	c	4.53
World Total	8,048.4	25.9	100.0	4,893.8	100.0	25.3	24.4	

a. Ratio of exports to domestic production.
b. Ratio of imports to domestic production.
c. Less than 0.1 percent.
n.a. = Not available.
Source: van der Merwe, Rowena, and others. *The Supply-side Effects of Tobacco Control Policies.* Background paper. (Data are compiled from U.S. Department of Agriculture, the Food and Agricultural Organization, and other sources.)

Republic, Macedonia, Kyrgyzstan, and Tanzania—rely heavily on tobacco as a source of foreign exchange, although their shares of the global tobacco-growing market are small. Tobacco is a major earner for a few countries with heavily agrarian economies, including Malawi, Zimbabwe, India, and Turkey.

Historically, tobacco is a highly attractive crop to farmers, providing a higher net income yield per unit of land than most cash crops and substantially more than food crops. In the best tobacco-growing areas of Zimbabwe, for example, tobacco is approximately 6.5 times more profitable than the next-best alternative crop. Farmers also find tobacco an attractive crop for more practical reasons. First, the global price of tobacco is relatively stable compared with other crops. The stability allows farmers to plan ahead and obtain credit for other enterprises as well as tobacco farming. Second, the tobacco industry generally supplies farmers with strong in-kind support, including materials and advice. Third, the industry often gives farmers loans. Fourth, other crops may cause farmers problems with storage, collection, and delivery. Tobacco is less perishable than many crops, and the industry may assist with its delivery or collection; by contrast, late collection, late payment, and price fluctuations may blight other crops.

There have been a number of experimental schemes to substitute other crops for tobacco. However, with the arguable exception of Canada, there is no hard evidence that these schemes succeed as a means of reducing tobacco consumption, because of the lack of motivation for farmers to participate while current tobacco prices persist and because of the readiness of other suppliers to replace them. Crop substitution will, however, occasionally have a place in broader diversification programs, if it aids the poorest tobacco farmers in their transition to other livelihoods. We discuss this issue in more detail in the next chapter.

Price supports and subsidies on tobacco production

While developing countries tend to tax export earnings from tobacco, high-income countries such as the United States and member states of the European Union, together with China, traditionally provide price supports and other subsidies to farmers who grow it. The motives for subsidizing tobacco production include keeping prices high and stable, supporting small family farms, controlling imports of tobacco from abroad to conserve foreign exchange, and maintaining political support. Often these subsidies go hand in hand with import restrictions.

With these price-support policies for producers, high-income countries' governments artificially raise world prices of tobacco and tobacco products. Economists have argued that, whenever the price is raised in this way, smokers may respond by reducing their consumption. However, the evidence shows that if there is such an effect on consumption, it is very small. In most high-income countries such as the United States, the producer price of tobacco leaf accounts for only a small part of the price of cigarettes. In addition, imports of lower-priced tobacco are rising. Thus, such price supports and subsidies will make only a negligible difference to the price of a pack. A recent analysis indicates that these programs raise prices by 1 percent in the United States. An increase of this order will have almost no impact on consumption. Accordingly, the removal of subsidies is unlikely to cause significant increases in cigarette consumption.

It is not clear how the removal of price supports and subsidies would affect global production. Higher domestic prices in the United States may help to raise the global price of raw tobacco leaf, offering better returns to farmers in low-income countries. On the other hand, there would be mixed effects for farmers in low-income countries if both subsidies and trade restrictions were removed. If, for example, the price of domestically produced tobacco in the United States were to fall because of the removal of subsidies, cigarette manufacturers there might use more of it, in turn reducing their imports of lower quality imports from low-income countries. But at the same time, with freer trade, imports of such tobacco could increase.

Regardless of their minimal impact on consumption, such price supports and subsidies make little sense in a framework of sound agricultural and trade policies. Their most significant function is perhaps political, enlarging the number of people with a vested interest in tobacco production.

Restrictions on international trade

Free trade has been shown to increase consumers' options and make production more efficient. A number of studies have shown that it brings increased growth to low-and middle-income countries. While the arguments in favor of free trade in general, then, are robust, tobacco is clearly more harmful to health than most other traded consumer goods. The key issue for policymakers is to decide how to control tobacco without jeopardizing the otherwise beneficial consequences of free trade. As we saw in chapter 1, trade liberalization has contributed to an increase in the consumption of tobacco in low- and middle-income countries. It might appear logical that, in turn, trade restrictions would stem that increase. However, there are a number of reasons why such restrictions would have undesirable consequences. One key reason is that restrictions would be likely to prompt retaliatory action that could reduce economic growth and incomes. Trade liberalization, meanwhile, has resulted in an international response through the General Agreement on Tariffs and Trade (GATT) that gives countries the right to adopt and enforce measures to protect public health. The condition for such measures is that they should be applied equally to domestic and imported products. Article XX of GATT explicitly states that measures that are needed to protect human health shall not be prevented by the requirement for free trade.

In 1990, Thailand attempted to ban cigarette imports and advertising, a move that prompted a challenge from U.S. tobacco companies. A GATT panel investigated the situation and ruled that Thailand could not ban imports of cigarettes, but that it could impose taxes, advertising bans, and price restrictions, and that it could demand that all manufacturers whose products were available in Thailand should label their products with strong warning labels and descriptions of the ingredients. The GATT panel's ruling has even been interpreted as saying that Thailand could ban sales of *all* tobacco products in the country, provided the ban were applied symmetrically to domestically produced and foreign-produced cigarettes. Thailand implemented strong demand-reduction measures, including comprehensive bans on advertising and promotion, and strong warning labels on cigarette packs. This landmark decision, and Thailand's prompt and firm response, have set a precedent for countries to intervene to reduce tobacco demand on public health grounds while maintaining the principles of free trade.

Firm action on smuggling

Cigarette smuggling is a serious problem. Researchers estimate that some 30 percent of internationally exported cigarettes, or about 355 billion cigarettes, are lost to smuggling. This is a far higher percentage than most consumer goods that are internationally traded. The problem is acute where there are large variations in tax between neighboring states or countries, where there is widespread corruption, and where contraband sales are tolerated. Here, we briefly describe the extent of the smuggling problem and discuss the options for its control. The benefit of controlling smuggling is not principally that it reduces supply, but that it helps the effective implementation of price increases that reduce demand.

Differences in price between countries or states will clearly increase the incentives to smuggle cigarettes. However, the determinants of smuggling appear to be more than price alone. A study prepared for this report assessed the extent to which other factors, such as general levels of corruption in a country, contribute to the size of the smuggling problem. Using standard indicators of corruption levels based on Transparency International's Index of Countries, the study concluded that, with notable exceptions, the level of tobacco smuggling tends to rise in line with the degree of corruption in a country (Figure 5.1).

Large-scale tobacco smuggling relies on criminal organizations, comparatively sophisticated systems for distributing smuggled cigarettes in the destination country, and a lack of control on the international movement of cigarettes. Most smuggled cigarettes are well-known international brands. Significant sums

FIGURE 5.1   TOBACCO SMUGGLING TENDS TO RISE IN LINE WITH THE
DEGREE OF CORRUPTION
Smuggling as a function of transparency index

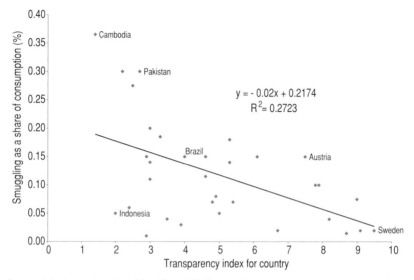

Source: Merriman, David, A. Yurekli, and F. Chaloupka. "How Big Is the Worldwide Cigarette Smuggling Problem?" NBER Working Paper. Cambridge, Mass.: National Bureau of
Economic Research, forthcoming.

of money are involved: organized smugglers can buy a container of 10 million
cigarettes, on which they pay no taxes, for $200,000. The fiscal value of this
quantity of cigarettes in the European Union is at least $1 million, taking ac-
count of excise duties, value-added tax (VAT), and import taxes. The profits to
smugglers are thus so high that they can absorb long-distance travel costs.

Cigarettes are usually smuggled in transit between their country of origin
and their official destination. To encourage trade between countries, a so-called
transit system operates that temporarily suspends custom duties, excise, and
VAT payable on goods originating in country A and bound for country B while
they are in transit through countries C, D, and so on. However, many cigarettes
simply fail to arrive at their destination, having been bought and sold by unof-
ficial traders. Another form of smuggling is so-called "round-tripping" where
there are relatively large price differentials between neighboring countries.
Exported cigarettes from Canada, Brazil, and South Africa, for example, have
been documented entering neighboring countries and then reappearing in their
country of origin at cut-rate prices, untaxed.

The success of smuggling relies on the cigarettes passing through a large number of owners in a short time, making it virtually impossible to track their movements. Additionally, poor enforcement of illegal sales and difficulty in separating legal and illegal sales may reduce the risks to smugglers. For example, in Russia, and in many low-income countries, the majority of cigarettes are sold on the streets.

Economic theory suggests that the tobacco industry itself will benefit from the existence of smuggling. Studies of the impact of smuggling show that when smuggled cigarettes account for a high percentage of the total sold, the average price for all cigarettes, taxed and untaxed, will fall, increasing sales of cigarettes overall. The presence of smuggled cigarettes in a market that has hitherto been closed to imported brands will help to increase the demand for those brands, and hence increase their market share. It will also influence governments toward keeping tax rates low.

There is as yet very little experience and research on the effectiveness of different antismuggling measures. However, policymakers may consider several options. First, the legality or otherwise of cigarette packs could be made more immediately visible to consumers and law enforcers by, for example, the addition of prominent tax stamps—which must be difficult to forge—on duty-paid packs, and special packaging on duty-free packs. Strong and varied warning labels in local languages also help to distinguish legal from illegal sales. Second, the penalties for smuggling could be made sufficiently severe to deter those who currently perceive the risks of prosecution to be low. Third, all parties in the chain between manufacturer and consumer could be licensed. This is already the case in France and Singapore. Fourth, manufacturers could be required to stamp each pack of cigarettes with a serial number to enable tracking. With increasingly sophisticated technology, pack marking could provide information about the distributor, wholesaler, and exporter, too. Fifth, manufacturers could be required to take responsibility for better record-keeping to ensure the final destination of their products is as officially intended. Computerized control systems would enable governments to track individual consignments and inspect their progress at any time. Such a system is already in place in Hong Kong, China. Sixth, exporters could be required to label packs with the name of the country of final destination, and print health warnings in the language of that country. Where international companies produce their cigarettes locally, this could also be stated on the pack, to aid detection and increase awareness of smuggled cigarettes. A number of countries are stepping up their antismuggling activities. For example, the United Kingdom recently announced a package worth more than $55 million to combat the smuggling of tobacco and alcohol, including the provision of new dedicated staff posts. As experience grows, the prospects for better controls in all affected countries are likely to improve.

CHAPTER 6

The Costs and Consequences of
Tobacco Control

DESPITE the obvious threat from tobacco to global health, many governments, particularly in low- and middle-income countries, have not taken significant action to reduce its toll. In some cases, this is because the scale of the threat is underestimated, or because of a mistaken belief that little can be done to reduce consumption. However, many governments have hesitated to act because of concerns that tobacco control will have undesirable economic consequences. In this chapter, we discuss some common concerns about the consequences of tobacco control for economies and for individuals, and then assess the cost-effectiveness of interventions.

Will tobacco control harm the economy?

We briefly discuss some of the common concerns in turn, in the form of answers to some of the most frequently asked questions.

If demand for tobacco falls, will there be massive job losses?

A major reason for governments' inaction over tobacco is their fear of creating unemployment. This fear is derived mainly from the arguments of the tobacco industry, which says that control measures will result in millions of job losses across the world. Yet a closer inspection of the arguments, and the data on which they are based, suggests that the negative effects of tobacco control on employment have been greatly overstated. Tobacco production is a small part of most economies. For all but a very few agrarian countries heavily dependent on tobacco farming, there would be no *net* loss of jobs, and there might even be job gains if global tobacco consumption fell. This is because money once spent on tobacco would be spent on other goods and services, thereby generating more jobs. Even the handful of tobacco-dependent economies will have a market big enough to ensure their jobs for many years to come, even in the face of gradually declining demand.

The tobacco industry estimates that 33 million people are engaged in tobacco farming worldwide. This total includes seasonal workers, part-time workers, and family members of farmers. It also includes farmers who grow other products in addition to tobacco. Of the total, some 15 million are in China, and another 3.5 million in India. Zimbabwe has some 100,000 tobacco farm workers. Relatively small but still significant numbers are employed in the high-income countries: the United States, for example, has 120,000 tobacco farms, and the European Union has 135,000—mostly small—farms in Greece, Italy, Spain, and France. The manufacturing side of the tobacco industry is only a small source of jobs, as it is highly mechanized. In most countries tobacco manufacturing jobs account for well below 1 percent of total manufacturing employment. There are a few important exceptions to this pattern, with Indonesia relying on tobacco manufacturing for 8 percent of its total manufacturing output, and Turkey, Bangladesh, Egypt, the Philippines, and Thailand relying on it for between 2.5 and 5 percent of theirs. On the whole, though, it is clear that tobacco production is a small part of most economies.

Statements that tobacco controls will mean massive job losses are usually based on studies funded by the tobacco industry that estimate the number of jobs attributable to tobacco in each sector, the incomes associated with these jobs, tax revenues generated by tobacco sales, and the contribution of tobacco to the country's trade balance wherever this is relevant. These studies also estimate the multiplier effect of money earned in tobacco farming and manufacturing in stimulating activity elsewhere in the economy. However, the methods used for these studies have been criticized. First, they assess the *gross* contribution of tobacco to employment and the economy. Rarely, if ever, do they take account of the fact that if people stop spending money on tobacco, they usually spend it on other things instead, thus generating alternative jobs to compensate. Second, their methods overstate the impact of any intervention that reduces demand because their estimates of certain variables, such as trends in smoking and trends in the mechanization of cigarette production, tend to be static.

Independent studies of the impact of tobacco on individual economies reach different conclusions. Rather than consider the gross economic contribution of tobacco to the economy, the independent studies estimate its *net* contribution, that is, the benefit to the economy of all tobacco-related activity *after* taking into account the compensating effect of alternative jobs that would be generated by the money not spent on tobacco. The conclusions of these studies are that tobacco control policies would have little or no negative effect on total employment, except in a very few tobacco-producing countries.

A study in the United Kingdom found that jobs would increase by more than 100,000 full-time equivalents in 1990 if former smokers spent their money on luxury items, and if any decline in tax revenues brought about by nontax measures to reduce demand were offset by taxing other goods and services. A study in the United States found that the number of jobs would rise by 20,000 between 1993 and 2000 if all domestic consumption was eliminated. While there would be net job losses in the to-bacco-growing region of the United States, the national total would rise because of the money freed up from tobacco purchases and injected into other areas of the economy. Of course, industry transitions can be difficult and may create social and political problems in the short term. But economies go through many such transitions, and this one would not be exceptional.

The findings are not restricted to the high-income countries. Indeed, there are some low-income countries that might experience striking benefits. For example, according to a background study for this report, Bangladesh, whose cigarettes are almost all imported, would benefit markedly if all domestic consumption were eliminated. Within the formal sector of its economy, there could be a net gain in jobs of as much as 18 percent if smokers spent their money on other goods and services.

The impact on economies of a global fall in tobacco consumption will vary, depending on the type of economy. Countries can be grouped into three categories. The first category comprises countries that produce more raw tobacco than they consume, that is, net exporters. Examples include Brazil, Kenya, and Zimbabwe. The second category comprises countries that consume about as much as they produce, that is, so-called "balanced" tobacco economies. The third category consists of countries that consume more than they produce, meaning net and full importers. The latter category includes the highest number of countries by far, encompassing countries such as Indonesia, Nepal, and Vietnam.

For the biggest group of countries, net and full importers, much of the impact of tobacco controls is borne by consumers, and more jobs are likely to be created than are lost (Table 6.1). However, the small number of agrarian countries that are heavily dependent on tobacco could experience net national job losses. Among the worst-affected producer countries would be those that export most of their crop, such as Malawi and Zimbabwe. One model suggests that in Zimbabwe, if all domestic tobacco farming stopped tomorrow, there would be a net loss of 12 percent of jobs. It should be stressed, however, that such an extreme scenario is unlikely.

At the level of households and small rural communities, such adjustment would mean loss of income, upheaval, and possibly relocation, and many governments would consider it important to help ease the transition process (see Box 6.1).

TABLE 6.1. STUDIES ON THE EMPLOYMENT EFFECTS OF REDUCED OR ELIMINATED TOBACCO CONSUMPTION

Type of country and name and year	Net change in employment as a percentage of economy in base year given	Assumptions
Net Exporters		
Canada (1992)	0.1%	Elimination of all domestic consumption expenditures according to "average" expenditure patterns
United States (1993)	0%	Elimination of all domestic consumption expenditures according to "average" expenditure patterns
United Kingdom (1990)	+0.5%	Reduction in tobacco consumption expenditures by 40%, spending according to "recent stopper" expenditure patterns
Zimbabwe (1980)	-12.4%	Elimination of all domestic tobacco consumption and production, redistributed according to "average" input-output patterns
Balanced Tobacco Economies		
South Africa (1995)	+0.4%	Elimination of all domestic tobacco consumption expenditures, spending according to "recent stopper" expenditure patterns
Scotland (1989)	+0.3%	Elimination of all domestic tobacco consumption expenditures, spending according to "average" expenditure patterns
Net Importers		
Michigan State, U.S. (1992)	+0.1%	Elimination of all domestic tobacco consumption expenditures, spending according to "average" expenditure patterns
Bangladesh (1994)	+18.7%	Elimination of all domestic tobacco consumption expenditures, spending according to "average" expenditure patterns

Sources: Buck, David, and others, 1995; Irvine, I. J. and W. A. Sims, 1997; McNicoll, I. H. and S. Boyle, 1992; van der Merwe, Rowena, and others, background paper; Warner, K. E., and G. A. Fulton, 1994; Warner, K. E., and others, 1996.

BOX 6.1 HELP FOR THE POOREST FARMERS

There is little prospect of a sharp and sudden reduction in tobacco production. As the previous chapter showed, it is highly unlikely that supply-side policies to restrict tobacco production would be practicable or politically acceptable for the majority of countries. If *demand* for tobacco falls, meanwhile, it will fall slowly, allowing for an equally slow process of adjustment for those most directly affected.

An accurate assessment of the way in which gradually falling demand will affect tobacco-farming communities is clearly critical for policymakers. Studies in most high-income countries suggest that the economies of these countries' tobacco-growing areas have become gradually diversified. In high-income countries, tobacco farmers have been making economic adjustments for decades, and many tobacco farm communities can draw on more diversified economies today than in the past. Interest in further diversification is common. A recent survey of tobacco farmers in the United States indicates, for example, that half of those questioned were at least aware of profitable alternative agricultural activities being pursued by other tobacco farmers in their own counties. Younger and more educated farmers were more likely than older farmers to be interested in diversification, and more likely to view diversification as possible. Likewise, a sizable minority of farmers questioned in the survey were aware of the prospect of change but recognized that it would be slow. Although more than eight out of 10 said that they personally expected to remain in tobacco farming, one in three said they would advise their children not to remain in the same business.

Nonetheless, there are several reasons why governments would want to provide assistance to meet the transition costs for their poorest farmers. Farms are a major source of rural employment and are often viewed as socially important by many societies. In addition, farmers can represent significant political opposition to tobacco control. Appropriate action for governments would involve a number of different efforts, such as encouraging sound agricultural and trade policies, the provision of broad rural development programs, assistance with crop diversification, rural training, and other safety-net systems. Some governments have proposed that such support could be financed out of tobacco taxes. Governments may also learn from the success of local efforts. In the United States, for instance, some rural communities that are traditionally dependent on tobacco have formed coalitions with public health constituencies to agree upon core principles for policies that will reduce tobacco consumption and also promote sustainable rural communities.

Will higher tobacco taxes reduce government revenues?

Policymakers frequently argue against raising tobacco taxes on the basis that the resulting reduction in demand will cost governments vital revenue. In fact, the reverse is true in the short to medium term, even though the situation in the very long term is less certain. Tax revenues can be expected to rise in the short to medium term because, although higher prices clearly reduce consumption, the demand for cigarettes is relatively inelastic. So cigarette consumption will fall, but by a smaller proportion than prices will rise. In the United Kingdom, for example, cigarette taxes have been raised repeatedly over the past three decades. Partly because of these increases, and partly because of the steady increase in awareness about the health consequences of smoking, consumption has declined sharply over the same period, with the annual number of cigarettes sold falling from 138 billion to 80 billion over three decades. Revenues, however, are still rising. For every tax increase of 1 percent in the United Kingdom, government revenues increase by between 0.6 and 0.9 percent (see Figure 6.1). A model developed for this study concludes that modest increases in cigarette excise taxes of 10 percent worldwide would increase tobacco tax revenues by about 7 percent overall, with the effects varying by country.

Some nonprice measures, such as advertising and promotion bans, mass information, and warning labels, would be expected to reduce revenue. Interventions to liberalize nicotine replacement therapy and other cessation efforts would also reduce consumption, and thus revenue. However, any such impact on revenue would be gradual, and a comprehensive control package that includes tax increases is in any case likely to lead to net revenue increases.

It is of course important to recognize that, if the ultimate aim of tobacco control is to benefit human health, then ideally the policymaker might wish to see tobacco consumption fall to such low levels that, eventually, tobacco tax revenues would begin to fall, too. This ultimate loss of revenue could be considered as the measure of success of tobacco control—or society's willingness to pay for the health benefits of reduced smoking. But this is a theoretical possibility rather than a probable scenario. Based on current patterns, the number of smokers is expected to grow in low-income countries over the next three decades. Equally important, governments would be free to introduce an alternative income tax or consumption tax that would replace the revenue from tobacco taxes.

Will higher tobacco taxes cause massive increases in smuggling?

It has been argued that higher taxes will contribute to increased cigarette smuggling and associated criminal activity. In this scenario cigarette consumption will remain high and tax revenues will fall. However, econometric and other

FIGURE 6.1   AS TOBACCO TAX RISES, REVENUE RISES TOO
Real price and tobacco taxation revenue in the U.K., 1971–95

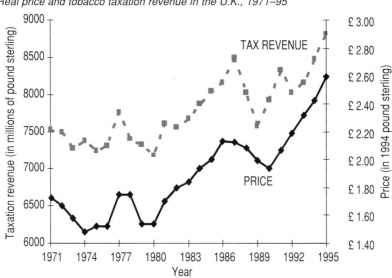

Source: Townsend, Joy. "The Role of Taxation Policy in Tobacco Control." In Abedian, I., and others, eds. *The Economics of Tobacco Control.* Cape Town, South Africa: Applied Fiscal Research Centre, University of Cape Town.

analyses of the experience of a large number of high-income countries show that, even in the face of high rates of smuggling, tax increases bring increased revenues and reduce cigarette consumption. Therefore, while smuggling is undoubtedly a serious problem, and while steep differentials in tobacco tax rates between countries are an incentive to smugglers, the appropriate response to smuggling is not to reduce tax rates or forego tax increases. Instead, it is more appropriate to crack down on crime. A second logical conclusion is that harmonization in cigarette tax rates between neighboring countries will help to reduce the incentives to smuggle.

Canada's experience illustrates these points clearly. In the early 1980s and 1990s, Canada increased its cigarette taxes sharply so that the real price rose significantly. Between 1979 and 1991 teenage smoking fell by nearly two-thirds, adult smoking declined, and cigarette tax revenues rose substantially. However, because of concerns about greatly increased smuggling, the government cut cigarette taxes sharply. In response, the prevalence of smoking climbed in teenagers, and also increased again in the population as a whole. Meanwhile federal tobacco tax revenues fell by more than twice as much as predicted.

The experience of South Africa is also illuminating. During the 1990s, South Africa increased its excise taxes on cigarettes sharply, by more than 450 percent. As a percentage of sale price, taxation rose from 38 to 50 percent. Not surprisingly, smuggling rose, too, from zero to about 6 percent of the market, the global average. Sales fell by more than 20 percent, implying a significant net fall in consumption even with increased smuggling. Meanwhile, total tax revenues more than doubled in real terms.

An econometric study assessed the potential impact of various different tax scenarios on the incentive for cigarette smuggling between countries in Europe. The analysis concluded that, even with rates of smuggling several times higher than those reported in Europe, higher taxes would still result in larger overall revenues. The study concluded that smuggling induced by price rises is likely to be a more significant problem in countries whose cigarettes are already priced high. Smuggling to countries with relatively cheap cigarettes would be relatively unaffected by price increases.

Will poor consumers bear the heaviest financial burden?

In many societies, there is a consensus that tax systems should be equitable, in the sense that those individuals with the greatest ability to pay should be taxed most heavily. This consensus is reflected, for example, in progressive income tax systems, where the marginal rates of tax rise as incomes rise. Tobacco taxes, however, are regressive, that is, like other consumption taxes on consumer goods, they place a disproportionately heavy financial burden on people with low incomes. This regressivity is further increased due to the fact that smoking is more common in poor households than rich households, so that poor smokers spend a larger share of their income on cigarette tax than do rich smokers.

There is concern that, as taxes are raised, poor consumers will spend more and more of their income on cigarettes, resulting in significant family hardship. Even with contracted demand, it is true that if poor consumers continue to consume more tobacco than the rich, they will also pay more tax. However, numerous studies show that people on lower incomes are more responsive to price changes than people on high incomes. As their consumption falls more steeply, their *relative* tax burden will fall compared with that of the richer consumer, even though their absolute payments will still be greater. Two studies from the United Kingdom and the United States support the idea of tobacco tax *increases* being progressive, even though tobacco tax in *itself* is regressive. Further studies in low- and middle-income countries are required to confirm this finding. Of course, all individual smokers will have to forego the perceived benefits of smoking and suffer the costs of withdrawal, and these losses will be comparatively greater for poor consumers.

Tobacco taxes, like any other single tax, need to work within the goal of ensuring that the *entire* system of tax and expenditure is proportional or progressive. Currently, the tax systems of most countries are a mix of many different taxes, where the overall goal is to be progressive or proportional, even though there may be individual taxes or elements of the system that are regressive. To offset the regressivity of a tobacco tax, governments could introduce more progressive taxes or other transfer programs. Provision of well-targeted social services, such as education and health programs, would tend to offset the regressivity of tobacco taxation.

While in principle public benefits should be financed out of general revenues, the unique ability of tobacco taxation to raise revenues cannot be ignored. In China, estimates suggest that a 10 percent increase in cigarette tax would decrease consumption by 5 percent and increase revenue by 5 percent, making the increase sufficient enough to finance a package of essential health services for one-third of China's poorest 100 million citizens.

Will tobacco control impose costs on individuals?

By reducing cigarette consumption, tobacco control measures will reduce the satisfaction, or benefits, of the smoker—just as curtailed consumption of any other consumer good reduces consumers' welfare. Regular smokers must either forego the pleasure of smoking, or incur the costs of quitting, or both. This is a loss of consumer surplus, and must be set against the gains of tobacco control.

However, as we saw earlier, tobacco is not a typical consumer good with typical benefits because of addiction and information problems. For the addicted smoker who regrets smoking and expresses a desire to quit, the benefits of smoking probably include the avoidance of withdrawal. If tobacco control measures reduce individual smokers' consumption, those smokers will face significant withdrawal costs.

Given that most regular smokers express a desire to quit but few are successful on their own, it seems likely that the perceived costs of quitting are greater than the perceived costs of continuing to smoke, such as damage to health. By making the costs of continued smoking greater than the costs of withdrawal, higher taxes can induce some smokers to quit. However, these smokers would still face withdrawal costs. Provision of information about the health consequences of smoking would increase the perceived costs of continuing to smoke, and alert smokers to the benefits of quitting. Widened access to nicotine replacement therapy (NRT) and other cessation interventions would help to reduce the costs of quitting.

It might be argued that tobacco control measures will impose bigger costs on poor individuals than on those with higher incomes. But if this is true for tobacco, it is certainly not unique in the field of public health. Compliance with many health interventions, such as child immunization or family planning, is often more costly for poor households. For example, poor families may have to walk longer distances to clinics than rich families, and may lose income in the process. Yet health officials do not usually hesitate to argue that the health benefits of most interventions, such as immunization, are worth the cost, provided the costs do not rise so high that poorer individuals are deterred from using services.

In considering the loss of consumer surplus to smokers, it is important to distinguish between regular smokers and others. For children and adolescents who are either beginners or merely potential smokers, the costs of avoiding tobacco are likely to be less severe, since addiction may not yet have taken hold and therefore withdrawal costs should be minimal. Other costs may include, for example, reduced acceptance by peers, less satisfaction from rebelling against parents, and the curtailment of other pleasures of smoking.

Restrictions on smoking in public places and private workplaces also impose costs on smokers by forcing them outdoors to smoke or reducing their opportunities to smoke. These interventions would appropriately shift the costs of smoking from nonsmokers to smokers. Again, for some, this increase in costs will lead them to change their smoking patterns and will impose costs. For nonsmokers, however, tobacco control policies will bring welfare gains. Clearly, welfare losses are likely to be minimized if control interventions are implemented as a package.

Is tobacco control worth paying for?

We now ask whether tobacco control is cost-effective relative to other health interventions. For governments considering intervention, such information may be a further important factor in deciding how to proceed.

The cost-effectiveness of different health interventions can be evaluated by estimating the expected gain in years of healthy life that each will achieve in return for the requisite public costs needed to implement that intervention. According to the World Bank's 1993 World Development Report, *Investing in Health*, tobacco control policies are considered cost-effective and worthy of inclusion in a minimal package of healthcare. Existing studies suggest that policy-based programs cost about $20 to $80 per discounted year of healthy life saved (one disability-adjusted life year, or DALY).[1]

For this study, estimates were made of the cost-effectiveness of each of the demand-reducing interventions discussed in chapter 4: tax rises, a package of nonprice measures including advertising and promotion bans, wider health information and public smoking restrictions, and NRT. The findings may be of particular value to low- and middle-income countries in assessing the relative emphases on specific interventions that are likely to be appropriate for their own needs.

The estimates were made within the model described in Box 4.1. The model's assumptions and inputs are described in full in a background paper to this report. Some of the interventions, such as raising taxes or banning advertising and promotion, have zero or minimal costs, as these are "stroke-of-the pen" interventions. To be conservative, the model assigned substantial implementation and administrative costs, along with drug costs for NRT. These costs do not, however, include possible costs borne by individuals. The results (Table 6.2) suggest that tax increases are by far the most cost-effective intervention, and one that compares favorably with many health interventions. Depending on the assumptions made about the administrative costs of raising and monitoring higher tobacco taxes, the cost of implementing a tax increase of 10 percent could be less than $5 per DALY (and would be unlikely to be more than $17 per DALY) in low- and middle income countries. This represents cost-effectiveness values comparable to many health interventions financed by governments, such as child immunization. Nonprice measures may also be highly cost-effective for low- and middle-income countries. Depending on the assumptions on which the estimates are based, a package could be delivered for as little as $68 per DALY. This level of cost-effectiveness compares reasonably with several established interventions in public health, such as the package for the integrated management of the sick child, which has been estimated to cost between $30 and $50 per DALY in low-income countries and between $50 and $100 in middle-income countries.

TABLE 6.2 THE COST-EFFECTIVENESS OF TOBACCO CONTROL MEASURES
Values for various tobacco control interventions (U.S. dollars per DALY saved), by region.

Region	Price increases of 10 percent	Nonprice measures with effectiveness of 5 percent	NRT (publicly provided) with 25 percent coverage
East Asia and Pacific	3 to 13	53 to 212	338 to 355
Eastern Europe and Central Asia	4 to 15	64 to 257	227 to 247
Latin America and Caribbean	10 to 42	173 to 690	241 to 295
Middle East and North Africa	7 to 28	120 to 482	223 to 260
South Asia	3 to 10	32 to 127	289 to 298
Sub-Saharan Africa	2 to 8	34 to 136	195 to 206
Low/Middle Income	4 to 17	68 to 272	276 to 297
High Income	161 to 645	1,347 to 5,388	746 to 1,160

Note: For all calculations, a 3 percent discount rate has been used, and benefits have been projected over a 30-year period; for nonprice interventions, costs have been projected over a 30-year period. The ranges result from varying the delivery costs of the interventions from 0.005% to 0.02% of GNP per annum.
Source: Ranson, Kent, P. Jha, F. Chaloupka, and A. Yurekli. Effectiveness and Cost-effectiveness of Price Increases and Other Tobacco Control Policy Interventions. Background paper.

The study also assessed the likely cost-effectiveness of widening access to NRT. For these estimates, it was assumed that the cost of NRT would be met from public funds. The results suggest that governments would need to exercise suitable caution in conducting local cost-effectiveness analyses before considering direct public provision of these new therapies. It is important to note that liberalizing access alone is far more likely to be cost-effective, and that as effectiveness and the numbers of adults wishing to quit grows, so would the cost-effectiveness of NRT improve.

More research is clearly needed to identify the effectiveness of such packages, their likely cost-effectiveness in countries of different income levels, and the costs to individuals.

There are only rudimentary estimates of the costs of *implementing* a comprehensive tobacco control program. The evidence from the high-income countries suggests that such comprehensive programs can be delivered for very small sums of money. High-income countries with very comprehensive programs spend between 50¢ and $2.50 per capita per year on these programs. In this context, tobacco control in low-income and middle-income countries is likely to be affordable, even in countries where per capita public expenditure on health is extremely low. The World Bank's 1993 World Development Report, *Investing in Health,* estimated that to deliver an essential package of public health interventions that *includes* tobacco control, governments would need to spend $4 per capita in low-income countries and $7 in middle-income countries. As a fraction of the total, tobacco control would be small.

Note

1. A disability-adjusted year (DALY) is a time-based measure that allows epidemiologists to capture in a single indicator the years of life lost to premature death (where premature death is defined as one that occurs before the age to which the dying person could have expected to survive if they were a member of a standardized model population with a life expectancy at birth equal to that of the world's longest-living population, in Japan) and years lived with a disability of a given severity and duration. One DALY is one lost year of healthy life.

CHAPTER 7

An Agenda for Action

ONLY two causes of death are large and growing worldwide: HIV and tobacco. While most countries have begun, at least, to respond to HIV, the response to the global tobacco epidemic has so far been limited and patchy. In this chapter, we discuss some of the factors that might influence governments' decisions to act and propose an agenda for effective action.

All governments recognize that, in forming their policies, they take account of many factors, and not only economics. Tobacco control policies are no exception. Most societies are concerned about protecting children, although the degree to which this is true varies from culture to culture. Most societies would wish to reduce the suffering and emotional losses wrought by tobacco's burden of disease and premature death. Economic studies have not yet brought any consensus to valuing that burden. For the policymaker seeking to improve public health, tobacco control is an attractive option. Even modest reductions in a disease burden of such large size would bring highly significant health gains. The consensus between societies that health gains are desirable is reflected in the tobacco policies and actions of the World Health Organization and in other international organizations (see Boxes 7.1 and 7.2 and Appendix A).

Many societies might consider that the strongest reason for acting to control tobacco is to deter children and adolescents from smoking. However, as the discussion in chapter 3 made clear, interventions that would specifically target only the youngest consumers are unlikely to have the desired effect, while those interventions that *are* effective—principally taxation—will also affect adults. Similarly, interventions designed specifically to protect nonsmokers would fail to protect most of them, and, once again, taxation would be the most effective option. In the context of real policymaking, many societies would consider the broader effects of these policies to be acceptable and, in pragmatic terms, even desirable. In any case, any tobacco control policy whose effect was solely to deter children from starting to smoke would have no impact on global smoking-related deaths for many decades, since most of the projected deaths for the first half of the next century are those of existing smokers (Figure 7.1). Therefore, governments concerned with health gains in the medium term would likely wish to encourage adults to quit also.

FIGURE 7.1   UNLESS CURRENT SMOKERS QUIT, TOBACCO DEATHS WILL RISE DRAMATICALLY IN THE NEXT 50 YEARS
Estimated cumulative tobacco deaths 1950–2050 with different intervention strategies

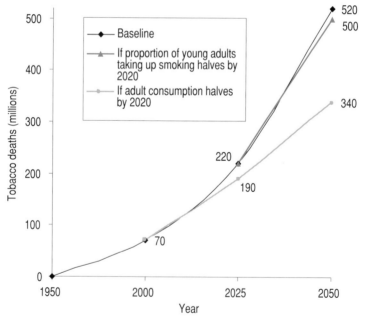

Note: Peto and others estimate 60 million tobacco deaths between 1950 and 2000 in developed countries. We estimate an additional 10 million between 1990 and 2000 in developing countries. We assume no tobacco deaths before 1990 in developing countries and minimal tobacco deaths worldwide before 1950. Projections for deaths from 2000 are based on Peto (personal communication [1998]).
Sources: Peto, Richard and others. 1994. *Mortality from Smoking in Developed Countries 1950–2000.* Oxford University Press; and Peto, Richard, personal communication.

Overcoming political barriers to change

To be effective, any government that decides to implement tobacco controls must do so in a context in which the decision has broad popular support. While it might seem that smokers would be strongly opposed to tobacco control, the reality is rather different: in studies of high-income countries with successful tobacco control programs, most adult smokers have been found to support at least some controls, such as widely available information. Governments alone cannot achieve success without the involvement of civil society, the private sector, and interest groups. Programs are more likely to succeed if there is collective agreement in and ownership of them across a broad coalition of social interests with the power to implement and sustain change.

There have been few attempts to quantify the combined impact of a mix of interventions. As chapter 4 showed, each individual intervention is capable of preventing millions of deaths, but whether a package of measures would save even more lives than the sum of each individual intervention together is as yet unknown. In implementing a package, each country would probably give different emphasis to different interventions, depending on the country's circumstances. For example, a country whose cigarette tax rates are currently lower than those of its neighbors is likely to see a particularly strong effect of tax increases on cigarette consumption. Similarly, a relatively well-educated and affluent population will respond less to price, and more to new information, than less educated and poorer populations. Cultural factors, such as a history of totalitarian rule, might also affect the ease with which some measures, such as smoking bans in public places, are accepted. These generalizations are simplistic, but policymakers may find them a useful starting point.

Governments contemplating action to control tobacco face major political obstacles to change. Yet, by identifying the key stakeholders on both the supply and demand sides in each country, policymakers can assess the size of each constituency, whether it is dispersed or concentrated, and other factors that may affect the constituency's response to change. For example, policymakers might note that winners, such as nonsmokers, may be a scattered and dispersed group, while losers, such as tobacco farmers, may have a powerful political and emotional voice. Careful planning and political mapping would be essential to achieve a smooth transition from reliance on tobacco to independence from it, whatever the nature of the economy and the national political framework. Such mapping exercises have been conducted, for example, in Vietnam.

Research priorities

Demand-reducing measures such as higher taxes and bans on advertising and promotion have already been seen to work in high-income countries, and enough is known already to implement these measures without delay. At the same time, however, a concurrent research agenda, both in epidemiology and economics, will be needed to help governments to adjust their packages of interventions to achieve the greatest chance of success. Some key research areas are outlined below.

Research into the causes, consequences, and costs of smoking at national and regional levels

Research is needed at national and regional levels to "count the tobacco dead" and classify deaths by cause. A simple and low-cost measure is to place questions on past smoking on death certificates, permitting comparisons of smoking excess among tobacco-attributable and other deaths. The benefits of such research go farther than their practical value of informing governments of the status of their tobacco epidemic or a baseline against which to monitor the impact of control efforts. They stimulate policy responses and may have a significant impact on tobacco consumption.

While epidemiological research into the consequences of smoking has at least begun to spread outside the high-income countries, research into the causes of smoking, the addictive nature of tobacco use, and the behavioral factors associated with smoking uptake remains heavily biased toward North America and Western Europe. While control interventions are being implemented, parallel research activities into these issues may help to refine the targeting of interventions, such as those designed to improve health information for the poor, for maximum effect.

For economists, research into the cost-effectiveness of each intervention at the national level is also a priority. Further data on price elasticity in low- and middle-income countries would be valuable, as would estimates of the social and healthcare costs of tobacco use in these countries.

Research into tobacco control has received less funding than might be expected in light of the size of the disease burden of smoking. During the early 1990s, the most recent time period for which data are available, investment in research and development in tobacco control amounted to $50 per 1990 death (a total of $148–$164 million). In contrast, HIV research and development received about $3,000 per 1990 death (a total of $919–$985 million). Spending on both diseases is concentrated primarily in high-income countries.

Recommendations

This report makes two recommendations:
   1. Where *governments* decide to take strong action to curb the tobacco epidemic, a multipronged strategy should be adopted. Its aims should be to deter children from smoking, to protect nonsmokers, and to pro-

vide all smokers with information about the health effects of tobacco. The strategy, tailored to individual country needs, would include: (1) raising taxes, using as a yardstick the rates adopted by countries with comprehensive tobacco control policies where consumption has fallen. In these countries, tax accounts for two-thirds to four-fifths of the retail price of cigarettes; (2) publishing and disseminating research results on the health effects of tobacco, adding prominent warning labels to cigarettes, adopting comprehensive bans on advertising and promotion, and restricting smoking in workplaces and public places; and (3) widening access to nicotine replacement and other cessation therapies.

2. *International organizations* such as the United Nations agencies should review their existing programs and policies to ensure that tobacco control is given due prominence; they should sponsor research into the causes, consequences, and costs of smoking, and the cost-effectiveness of interventions at the local level; and they should address tobacco control issues that cross borders, including working with the WHO's proposed Framework Convention for Tobacco Control. Key areas for action include facilitating international agreements on smuggling control, discussions on tax harmonization to reduce the incentives for smuggling, and bans on advertising and promotion involving the global communications media.

The threat posed by smoking to global health is unprecedented, but so is the potential for reducing smoking-related mortality with cost-effective policies. This report shows the scale of what might be achieved: moderate action could ensure substantial health gains for the 21st century.

BOX 7.1 THE WORLD HEALTH ORGANIZATION AND THE FRAMEWORK CONVENTION FOR TOBACCO CONTROL

At the World Health Assembly in May 1996, WHO's member states adopted a resolution calling upon the Director-General of WHO to initiate the development of a framework convention for tobacco control. WHO, under the leadership of Director-General Gro Harlem Brundtland, has assigned priority to reinvigorated work on tobacco control, and has established a new project, the Tobacco Free Initiative (TFI). A cornerstone of TFI's work is the WHO Framework Convention for Tobacco Control (FCTC).

The WHO FCTC would be an international legal instrument designed to circumscribe the growth of the global tobacco pandemic, especially in

(continued on next page)

BOX 7.1 (CONTINUED)

developing countries. If entered into force, the convention will be a first for WHO and a first for the world. This will be the first time that the 191 WHO member states exercise WHO's constitutional authority to serve as a platform for the development of a convention. In addition, this will be the first multilateral convention focusing specifically on a public health issue. The development of the WHO FCTC will be helped by knowledge of the addictive and lethal qualities of tobacco use, combined with many countries' interest to improve tobacco regulation through international instruments.

The international regulatory strategy being used to promote multilateral agreement and action on tobacco control is the framework convention-protocol approach. This strategy promotes global consensus in incremental stages by dividing the negotiation of separate issues into individual agreements:

- States first adopt a framework convention that calls for cooperation in achieving broadly stated goals and establishes the basic institutions of a multilateral legal structure.
- Separate protocol agreements containing specific measures designed to implement the broad goals called for by the framework convention.

The framework convention-protocol approach has been used to address other global problems, for example, the Vienna Convention for the Protection of the Ozone Layer and the Montreal Protocol.

The negotiation and implementation of the WHO FCTC would help to curb tobacco use by mobilizing national and international awareness as well as technical and financial resources for effective national tobacco control measures. The convention would also strengthen global cooperation on aspects of tobacco control that transcend national boundaries, including global marketing/promotion of tobacco products and smuggling. Though the negotiation of each treaty is unique and depends upon the political will of states, the WHO FCTC Accelerated Work Plan foresees adoption of the convention no later than May 2003.

BOX 7.2 THE WORLD BANK'S POLICY ON TOBACCO

The World Bank has since 1991 had a policy on tobacco, in recognition of its harmful effects on health. The policy contains five main points. First, the Bank's activities in the health sector, such as policy dialogue and lending, discourage the use of tobacco products. Second, the Bank does not lend directly for, invest in, or guarantee investment or loans for, tobacco production, processing, or marketing. However, in a few agrarian countries that are heavily dependent on tobacco as a source of income and of foreign exchange earnings, the Bank aims to deal with the issue by responding most effectively to these countries' development requirements. The Bank aims to help these countries diversify away from tobacco. Third, the Bank does not lend indirectly to tobacco production activities, to the extent that this is practicable. Fourth, tobacco and its related processing machinery and equipment cannot be included among imports financed under loans. Fifth, tobacco and tobacco-related imports may be exempt from borrowers' agreements with the Bank to liberalize trade and reduce tariffs.

The Bank's policy is consistent with the arguments for ending subsidies made in this report. However, the emphasis on supply-side measures has not reduced tobacco consumption in any measurable way from 1991 to today. In the interim, the Bank's work on tobacco control, comprising about 14 countries with total project costs of more than US$100 million, has largely been on health promotion and information. Extending this work to focus on pricing and regulation was supported in principle by the Bank's 1997 Sector Strategy Paper. This report confirms the importance of focusing on price as an effective means of reducing demand.

Tobacco Taxation: A View from the International Monetary Fund

INCREASES in tobacco excise rates are often included as a component of Fund-supported stabilization programs for countries that need to mobilize additional tax revenue to reduce the fiscal deficit. While excise rates on tobacco products may be increased primarily to raise revenue, there are also health benefits from reduced tobacco consumption.

In setting tobacco tax rates, governments need to take into account several factors, including the impact of smuggling, cross-border shopping, and duty-free purchases on ferries and planes. It is in the interest of governments to reduce tobacco smuggling not only to increase excise revenues but also to limit the loss of revenues from other taxes, including income and value-added taxes, as underground transactions replace legal ones. Ultimately, tobacco excise tax rates must reflect the purchasing power of the local consumers, rates in neighboring countries, and, above all, the ability and willingness of the tax authority to enforce compliance.

With respect to the structure of tobacco excises, countries should tax all types of tobacco—cigarettes, cigars, pipe tobacco, snuff or chewing tobacco, and hand-rolling tobacco. The best international practice is to impose excises on the destination basis under which imports are taxed and exports are freed of tax.

Excises can be either specific taxes (based on quantity) or ad valorem (based on value). If a primary purpose of the excise is to discourage tobacco consumption, a strong case can be made for specific excises that would impose the same tax per stick. Specific taxes also are easier to administer because it is only necessary to determine the physical quantity of the product taxed, and not necessary to determine its value. Ad valorem taxes, however, may keep pace with inflation better than specific taxes, even specific taxes that are adjusted fairly frequently.

The administration of domestic tobacco excises requires an integrated strategy for taxpayer registration; filing and payment; collection of overdue taxes; audit; and taxpayer services. Developing and transition countries may need to treat tobacco production facilities as extraterritorial and administer excises similar to customs duties. The tax authority would control shipments into and out of the production facility.

Excise stamps can assist in ensuring the payment of excises and ensuring that goods that have paid the tax appropriate for one jurisdiction are not shipped to another. Introduction of stamps, however, involves considerable costs for producers of excised goods. Stamps will serve little purpose in control unless their utilization is monitored at the retail level.

APPENDIX B

Background Papers

SOME of these background papers will be published in a forthcoming book by Oxford University Press titled *Tobacco Control Policies in Developing Countries,* edited by Prabhat Jha and Frank Chaloupka.

Bobak, Martin, Prabhat Jha, Son Nguyen, and Martin Jarvis. *Poverty and Tobacco.*

Chaloupka, Frank, Tei-Wei Hu, Kenneth E. Warner, Rowena van der Merwe, and Ayda Yurekli. *Taxation of Tobacco Products.*

Gajalakshmi, C.K., Prabhat Jha, Son Nguyen, and Ayda Yurekli. *Patterns of Tobacco Use, and Health Consequences.*

Jha, Prabhat, Phillip Musgrove, and Frank Chaloupka. *Is There a Rationale for Government Intervention?*

Jha, Prabhat, Fred Paccaud, Ayda Yurekli, and Son Nguyen. *Strategic Priorities for Governments and Development Agencies in Tobacco Control.*

Joossens, Luk, David Merriman, Ayda Yurekli, and Frank Chaloupka. *Issues in Tobacco Smuggling.*

Kenkel, Donald, Likwang Chen, Teh-Wei Hu, and Lisa Bero. *Consumer Information and Tobacco Use.*

Lightwood, James, David Collins, Helen Lapsley, Thomas Novotny, Helmut Geist, and Rowena van der Merwe. *Counting the Costs of Tobacco Use.*

Merriman, David, Ayda Yurekli, and Frank Chaloupka. *How Big Is the Worldwide Cigarette Smuggling Problem?*

Novotny, Thomas E., Jillian C. Cohen, and David Sweanor. *Smoking Cessa-*

tion, Nicotine Replacement Therapy, and the Role of Government in Supporting Cessation.

Peck, Richard, Frank Chaloupka, Prabhat Jha, and James Lightwood. *Cost-Benefit Analysis of Tobacco Consumption*.

Ranson, Kent, Prabhat Jha, Frank Chaloupka, and Ayda Yurekli. *Effectiveness and Cost-effectiveness of Price Increases and Other Tobacco Control Policy Interventions*.

Saffer, Henry. *The Control of Tobacco Advertising and Promotion*.

Sunley, Emil M., Ayda Yurekli, and Frank Chaloupka. *The Design, Administration, and Potential Revenue of Tobacco Excises: A Guide for Developing and Transition Countries*.

Taylor, Allyn L., Frank Chaloupka, Emmanuel Guindon, and Michaelyn Corbett. *Trade Liberalization and Tobacco Consumption*.

Van der Merwe, Rowena, Fred Gale, Thomas Capehart, and Ping Zhang. *The Supply-side Effects of Tobacco Control Policies*.

Woollery, Trevor, Samira Asma, Frank Chaloupka, and Thomas E. Novotny. *Other Measures to Reduce the Demand for Tobacco Products*.

Yurekli, Ayda, Son Nguyen, Frank Chaloupka, and Prabhat Jha. *Statistical Annex*.

Acknowledgments

THIS report benefited greatly from ideas, technical inputs, and critical review from a broad range of individuals and organizations. Contributions to specific chapters are acknowledged in the Bibliographical Note. Reviewers for the background papers or the summary report are noted below. In addition, valuable input was provided by a series of consultations.

A. Reviewers for Background Papers or the Summary Report

Iraj Abedian, Samira Asma, Peter Anderson, Enis Baris, Howard Barnum, Edith Brown-Weiss, Neil Collishaw, Michael Ericksen, Christine Godfrey, Robert Goodland, Ramesh Govindaraj, Vernor Griese, Jack Henningfield, Chee-Ruey Hsieh, Teh-Wei Hu, Gregory Ingram, Paul Isenman, Steven Jaffee, Dean Jamison, Michael Linddal, Alan Lopez, Dorsati Madani, Will Manning, Jacob Meerman, Cyril Muller, Philip Musgrove, Richard Peck, Richard Peto, Markku Pekurinen, John Ryan, David Sweanor, John Tauras, Joy Townsend, Adam Wagstaff, Kenneth Warner, Trevor Woollery, Russell Wilkins, Witold Zatonski, Barbara Zolty, and Mitch Zeller

B. Consultations

1. Examination of Draft Report Outline and Key Economic Issues

August 27, 1997, at the 10th World Conference on Tobacco or Health, Beijing, China. Supported by the World Bank.
Chair: Thomas Novotny

Participants: Iraj Abedian, Frank Chaloupka, Simon Chapman, Kishore Chaudhry, Neil Collishaw, Vera Luisa da Costa y Silva, Prakash Gupta, Laksmiati Hanafiah, Natasha Herrera, Teh-Wei Hu, Desmond Johns, Prabhat Jha, Luk Joossens, Ken Kyle, Eric LeGresley, Michelle Lobo, Judith Mackay, Patrick Masobe, Kathleen McCormally, Zofia Mielecka-Kubien, Rafael Olganov, Alex Papilaya, Terry Pechacek, Milton Roemer, Ruth Roemer, Lu Rushan, Cecilia Sepulveda, David Simpson, Paramita Sudharto, Joy Townsend, Sharad Vaidya, Rowena Van Der Merwe, Kenneth Warner, Shaw Watanabe, David Zaridze, and Witold Zatonski

2. Initial Review of Outlines and Content of Background Papers

February 20, 1998, at the University of Cape Town's conference on "The Economics of Tobacco: Toward an Optimal Policy Mix," Cape Town, South Africa. Supported by the Institute of Social and Preventive Medicine at the University of Lausanne, and the University of Cape Town.

Chair: Paul Isenman

Participants: Iraj Abedian, Judith Bale, Enis Baris, Frank Chaloupka, David Collins, Neil Collishaw, Brian Easton, Helmut Geist, Chee-Ruey Hsieh, Teh-Wei Hu, Prabhat Jha, Luk Joossens, Kamal Nayan Kabra, Pamphil Kweyuh, Helen Lapsley, Judith Mackay, Eddie Maravanyika, Sergiusz Matusia, Thomas Novotny, Fred Paccaud, Richard Peck, Krzysztof Przewozniak, Yussuf Saloojee, Conrad Shamlaye, Timothy Stamps, Krisela Steyn, Frances Stillman, David Sweanor, Joy Townsend, Rowena Van Der Merwe, Kenneth Warner, and Derek Yach

3. Economists Technical Review Meeting

November 22–24, 1998, in Lausanne, Switzerland. Sponsored by the Institute of Social and Preventive Medicine at the University of Lausanne, and the World Bank.

Co-Chairs: Felix Gutzwiller and Fred Paccaud

Participants: Iraj Abedian, Nisha Arunatilleke, Martin Bobak, Phyllida Brown, Frank Chaloupka, David Collins, Jacques Cornuz, Christina Czart, Nishan De Mel, Jean-Pierre Gervasoni, Peter Heller, Tomasz Hermanowski, Alberto Holly, Teh-Wei Hu, Paul Isenman, Dean Jamison, Prabhat Jha, Luk Joossens, Jim Lightwood, Helen Lapsley, David Merriman, Phillip Musgrove, Son Nam Nguyen, Richard Peck, Markku Pekurinen, Thomson Prentice, Kent Ranson, Marie-France Raynault, John Ryan, Henry Saffer, David Sweanor, John Tauras, Allyn Taylor, Joy Townsend, Rowena van der Merwe, Kenneth Warner, Trevor

Woollery, and Ayda Yurekli

4. External Experts Review

March 17, 1999, in Washington, D.C. Sponsored by the Office on Smoking and Health, U.S. Centers for Disease Control and Prevention.

Chair: Michael Ericksen

Participants: Iraj Abedian, Samira Asma, Judith Bale, Enis Baris, Phyllida Brown, Frank Chaloupka, Peter Heller, Paul Isenman, Prabhat Jha, Nancy Kaufman, Thomas Loftus, Judith Mackay, Caryn Miller, Rose Nathan, Son Nam Nguyen, Fred Paccaud, Anthony So, Roberta Walburn, Kenneth Warner, Trevor Woollery, Derek Yach, and Ayda Yurekli

APPENDIX D

The World by Income and Region (World Bank Classification)

East Asia and Pacific	Europe and Central Asia	Latin America and the Caribbean	Middle East and North Africa	South Asia	Sub-Saharan Africa	High-income OECD	Other high income
Low income							
Cambodia	Armenia	Guyana	Yemen, Rep.	Afghanistan	Angola		
China	Azerbaijan	Haiti		Bangladesh	Benin		
Lao PDR	Bosnia and	Honduras		Bhutan	Burkina Faso		
Mongolia	Herzegovina	Nicaragua		India	Burundi		
Myanmar	Kyrgyz Rep.			Nepal	Cameroon		
Vietnam	Moldova			Pakistan	Central African		
	Tajikistan			Sri Lanka	Rep.		
					Chad		
					Comoros		
					Congo, Dem. Rep.		
					Congo, Rep.		
					Côte d'Ivoire		
					Equatorial Guinea		
					Eritrea		
					Ethiopia		
					Gambia, The		
					Ghana		
					Guinea		
					Guinea-Bissau		
					Kenya		
					Lesotho		
					Liberia		

(Continues on next page)

The World by Income and Region (World Bank Classification) - *(continued)*

East Asia and Pacific	Europe and Central Asia	Latin America and the Caribbean	Middle East and North Africa	South Asia	Sub-Saharan Africa	High-income OECD	Other high income
Low income - (continued)							
					Madagascar		
					Malawi		
					Mali		
					Mauritania		
					Mozambique		
					Niger		
					Nigeria		
					Rwanda		
					São Tomé and Principe		
					Senegal		
					Sierra Leone		
					Somalia		
					Sudan		
					Tanzania		
					Togo		
					Uganda		
					Zambia		
					Zimbabwe		
Lower middle income							
Fiji	Albania	Belize	Algeria	Maldives	Botswana		
Indonesia	Belarus	Bolivia	Egypt, Arab		Cape Verde		
Kiribati	Bulgaria	Colombia	Iran, Islamic Rep.		Djibouti		
Korea, Dem. Rep	Estonia	Costa Rica	Iraq		Namibia		
Marshall Islands	Georgia Kazakstan	Cuba	Jordan		Swaziland		
		Dominica					

Micronesia Fed. Sts.	Latvia	Dominican Rep.	Lebanon	Gabon
Papua New Guinea	Lithuania	Ecuador	Morocco	Mauritius
Philippines	Macedonia, FYR	El Salvador	Syrian Arab Rep.	Mayotte
Samoa	Romania	Grenada	Tunisia	Seychelles
Solomon Islands	Russian Fed.	Guatemala	West Bank and Gaza	South Africa
Thailand	Turkey	Jamaica		
Tonga	Turkmenistan	Panama		
Vanuatu	Ukraine	Paraguay		
	Uzbekistan	Peru		
	Yugoslavia, Fed. Rep.	St. Vincent and the Grenadines		
		Suriname		
		Venezuela		

Upper middle income

American Samoa	Croatia	Antique and Barbuda	Bahrain	
Malaysia	Czech Rep.	Argentina	Libya	
Palau	Hungary	Barbados	Oman	
	Isle of Man	Brazil	Saudi Arabia	
	Malta	Chile		
	Poland	Guadeloupe		
	Slovak Rep.	Mexico		
	Slovenia	Puerto Rico		
		St. Kitts and Nevis		
		St. Lucia		
		Trinidad and Tobago		
		Uruguay		

(Continues on next page)

The World by Income and Region (World Bank Classification) - *(continued)*

East Asia and Pacific	Europe and Central Asia	Latin America and the Caribbean	Middle East and North Africa	South Asia	Sub-Saharan Africa	High-income OECD	Other high income
High income							
						Australia	Andorra
						Austria	Aruba
						Belgium	Bahamas, The
						Canada	Bermuda
						Denmark	Brunei
						Finland	Cayman Is.
						France	Channel Is.
						Germany	Cyprus
						Greece	Faeroe Is.
						Iceland	French
						Ireland	Guiana
						Italy	French
						Japan	Polynesia
						Korea, Rep.	Greenland
						Luxembourg	Guam
						Netherlands	Hong Kong,
						New Zealand	China
						Norway	Israel
						Portugal	Kuwait
						Spain	Liechtenstein
						Sweden	Macao
						Switzerland	Martinique
						United Kingdom	Monaco
						United States	Netherlands
							Antilles
							New Caledonia
							Northern
							Mariana Is.

Qatar
Reunion
Singapore
United Arab
  Emirates
Virgin Islands
  (U.S.)

Source: *World Bank, 1998*

Bibliographic Note

Chapter 1. Global Trends in Tobacco Use

The discussion on consumption and epidemiology draws upon Gajalakshmi and others, background paper; Lund and others, 1995; Ranson and others, background paper; Wald and Hackshaw, 1996, and World Health Organization, 1997. The section on socioeconomic status draws on Bobak and others, background paper; Chinese Academy of Preventive Medicine, 1997; Gupta, 1996; Jenkins and others, 1997; Obot, 1990; Hill and others, 1998; U.S. Surgeon General Reports, 1989 and 1994; the U.K. Government 1998; Wersall and Eklund, 1998; and White and Scollo, 1998. The discussion on trade liberalization draws upon Chaloupka and Laixuthai, 1996; and Taylor and others, background paper.

Chapter 2. The Health Consequences of Smoking

The discussion on nicotine addiction draws on Charlton, 1996; Foulds, 1996; Lynch and Bonnie, 1994; Kessler, 1995; McNeill, 1989; and the U.S. Surgeon General Reports 1988, 1989, and 1994. The discussion of the disease burden attributable to smoking draws on Bobak and others, background paper; Doll and Peto, 1981; Doll and others, 1994; Environmental Protection Agency, 1992; Gajalakshmi and others, background paper; Gupta, 1989; Jha and others, forthcoming; Liu and others, 1998; Meara, forthcoming; Niu and others, 1998; Parish and others, 1995; Peto and others, 1994; Peto, Chen, and Boreham, 1999; and Royal College of Physicians, 1992.

Chapter 3. Do Smokers Know Their Risks and Bear the Costs?

The discussion on awareness of health risks draws upon Ayanian and Cleary, 1999; Barnum, 1994; Chaloupka and Warner, in press; Chinese Academy of Preventive Medicine, 1997; Johnston and others, 1998; Kenkel and others, background paper; Kessler, 1995; Levshin and Droggachih, 1999; Schoenbaum, 1997; Viscusi, 1990, 1991, and 1992; Weinstein,1998 and Zatonski, 1996. The discussion of costs imposed on others draws on Lightwood and others, background paper, Manning and others, 1991; Pekurinen, 1992; Viscusi, 1995; Warner and others, in press; and World Bank 1994b.

Chapter 4. Measures to Reduce the Demand of Tobacco

This chapter draws on Abedian and others, 1998; Chaloupka and others, background paper; Chaloupka and Warner, in press; Townsend, 1996; Jha and others, background paper; Kenkel and others, background paper; Laugesen and Meads, 1991; Novotny and others, background paper; Pekurinen, 1992; Ranson and others, background paper; Raw and others, 1999; Reid, 1996; Saffer and Chaloupka, 1999; Saffer and others, background paper; Tansel, 1993; Townsend, 1998; U.K. Department of Health, 1998; U.S. Surgeon General Report, 1989; Warner and others, 1997; and Zatonski and others, 1999.

Chapter 5. Measures to Reduce the Supply of Tobacco

The chapter draws on Altman and others, 1998; Berkelman and Buehler, 1990; Chaloupka and Warner, in press; Crescenti, 1992; Food and Agriculture Organization, 1998; Ginsberg, 1999; IEC, 1998; Joossens and others, background paper; Maravanyika, 1998; Merriman and others, background paper; Reuter, 1992; Taylor and others, background paper; Thursby and Thursby, 1994; U.S. Department of Agriculture 1998; Van der Merwe, background paper; Warner, 1988; Warner and Fulton, 1994; Warner and others, 1996; and Zang and Husten, 1998.

Chapter 6. The Costs and Consequences of Tobacco Control Policies

This chapter draws on Altman and others, 1998; Buck and others, 1995; Centers for Disease Control and Prevention, 1998; Chaloupka and others, background paper; Doll and Crofton, 1996; Efroymson and others, 1996; Irvine and Sims, 1997; Jones, 1999; Joossens and others, background paper; McNicoll and Boyle, 1992; Murray and Lopez, 1996; Orphanides and Zervos, 1995; Suranovic and others, 1999; Townsend, 1998; Van der Merwe, 1998; Van der Merwe and others, background paper; Warner, 1987; Warner and Fulton, 1994; Warner and others, 1996; and World Bank, 1993.

Chapter 7. An Agenda for Action

This chapter draws on Jha and others, background paper; Abedian and others 1998; WHO 1996a; U.S. Surgeon General 1999; and Sanet and others 1997.

Bibliography

Abedian, Iraj, Rowena van der Merwe, Nick Wilkins, and Prabhat Jha, eds. 1998. *The Economics of Tobacco Control: Towards an Optimal Policy Mix.* Cape Town, South Africa: Applied Fiscal Reseach Centre, University of Cape Town.

Agro-economic Services, Ltd, and Tabacosmos, Ltd. 1987. *The Employment, Tax Revenue and Wealth that the Tobacco Industry Creates.*

Altman, D. G., D. J. Zaccaro, D. W. Levine, D. Austin, C. Woodell, B. Bailey, M. Sligh, G. Cohn, and J. Dunn. 1998. "Predictors of Crop Diversification: A Survey of Tobacco Farmers in North Carolina." *Tobacco Control* 7(4):376–82.

American Economics Group, Inc. 1996. *Economic Impact in the States of Proposed FDA Regulations Regarding the Advertising, Labeling and Sale of Tobacco Products.* Washington, D.C.

Atkinson, A. B., and J. L. Skegg. 1973. "Anti-Smoking Publicity and the Demand for Tobacco in the UK." *The Manchester School of Economic and Social Studies* 41:265–82.

Atkinson, A. B., J. Gomulka, and N. Stern. 1984. *Household Expenditure on Tobacco 1970-1980: Evidence from the Family Expenditure Survey.* London: London School of Economics.

Ayanian, J., and P. Cleary. 1999. "Perceived Risks of Heart Disease and Cancer Among Cigarette Smokers." *Journal of the American Medical Association* 281(11):1019–21.

Barendregt, J. J., L. Bonneux, and P. J. van der Maas. 1997. "The Health Care Costs of Smoking." *New England Journal of Medicine* 337(15):1052–7.

Barnum, Howard. 1994. "The Economic Burden of the Global Trade in Tobacco." *Tobacco Control* 3:358–61.

Barnum, Howard, and R. E. Greenberg. 1993. "Cancers." In Jamison, D. T, H. W Mosley, A. R. Measham, and J. L. Bobadilla, eds., *Disease Control Priorities in Developing Countries.* New York: Oxford Medical Publications.

Becker, G. S., M. Grossman, and K. M. Murphy. 1991. "Rational Addiction and the Effect of Price on Consumption." *American Economic Review* 81:237–41.

———. 1994. "An Empirical Analysis of Cigarette Addiction." *American Economic Review* 84:396-418.

Berkelman, R. L., and J. W. Buehler. 1990. "Public Health Surveillance of Non-Infectious Chronic Diseases: the Potential to Detect Rapid Changes in Disease Burden." *International Journal of Epidemiology* 19(3):628–35.

Booth, Martin. 1998. *Opium : A History.* New York: St. Martin's Press.

British American Tobacco. 1994. *Tobacco Taxation Guide: A Guide to Alternative Methods of Taxing Cigarettes and Other Tobacco Products.* Woking, U.K.: Optichrome The Printing Group.

Buck, David, C. Godfrey, M. Raw, and M. Sutton. 1995. *Tobacco and Jobs.* York, U.K.: Society for the Study of Addiction and the Centre for Health Economics, University of York.

Capehart, T. 1997. "The Tobacco Program—A Summary and Update." *Tobacco Situation & Outlook Report.* U.S. Department of Agriculture, Economic Research Service, TBS-238.

Chaloupka, F. J. 1990. *Men, Women, and Addiction: The Case of Cigarette Smoking.* NBER Working Paper No. 3267. Cambridge, Mass.: National Bureau of Economic Research.

———. 1991. "Rational Addictive Behavior and Cigarette Smoking." *Journal of Political Economy* 99(4):722–42.

———. 1998. *The Impact of Proposed Cigarette Price Increases.* Policy Analysis No. 9, Health Sciences Analysis Project. Washington D.C.: Advocacy Institute.

Chaloupka, F. J., and A. Laixuthai. 1996. *US Trade Policy and Cigarette Smoking in Asia*, NBER Working Paper No. 5543. Cambridge, Mass.: National Bureau of Economic Research.

Chaloupka, F. J., and H. Saffer. 1992. "Clean Indoor Air Laws and the Demand for Cigarettes." *Contemporary Policy Issues* 10(2):72–83.

Chaloupka, F. J., and H. Wechsler. 1997. "Price, Tobacco Control Policies and Smoking Among Young Adults." *Journal of Health Economics* 16(3):359–73.

Chaloupka, F. J., and K. E. Warner. In press. "The Economics of Smoking." In Newhouse, J., and A. Culyer, eds., *The Handbook of Health Economics*. Amsterdam: North Holland.

Chaloupka, F. J., and M. Grossman. 1996. *Price, Tobacco Control Policies and Youth Smoking*. NBER Working Paper No. 5740. Cambridge, Mass.: National Bureau of Economic Research.

Chaloupka, F. J., and R. L. Pacula. 1998. *An Examination of Gender and Race Differences in Youth Smoking Responsiveness to Price and Tobacco Control Policies*. NBER Working Paper No. 6541. Cambridge, Mass.: National Bureau of Economic Research.

Chalton, A. 1996. "Children and Smoking: The Family Circle." *British Medical Bulletin*, 52(1):90–107.

Chase Econometrics. 1985. *The Economic Impact of the Tobacco Industry on the United States Economy in 1983*. Bala Cynwyd, Penn.: Chase Econometrics.

Chinese Academy of Preventive Medicine. 1997. *Smoking in China: 1996 National Prevalence Survey of Smoking Pattern*. Beijing: China Science and Technology Press.

Coalition on Smoking or Health. 1994. *Saving Lives and Raising Revenue: The Case for a $2 Federal Tobacco Tax Increase*. Washington D.C.

Collins, D. J., and H. M. Lapsley. 1997. *The Economic Impact of Tobacco Smoking in Pacific Islands*. Wahroonga, NSW, Australia: Pacific Tobacco and Health Project.

Collishaw, Neil. 1996. "An International Framework Convention for Tobacco Control." *Heart Beat* 2:11.

Crescenti, M. G. 1992. "No Alternative to Tobacco." *Tobacco Journal International* 6, November-December 14.

Doll, Richard, and R. Peto. 1981. *The Causes of Cancer*. New York: Oxford University Press.

Doll, Richard, R. Peto, K. Wheatley, R. Gray, and I. Sutherland. 1994. "Mortality in Relation to Smoking: 40 Years' Observations on Male British Doctors." *British Medical Journal*, 309(6959):901–11.

Doll, Richard, and John Crofton, eds. 1996. "Tobacco and Health." *British Medical Bulletin* Vol. 52, No. 1.

Douglas, S. 1998. "The Duration of the Smoking Habit." *Economic Inquiry* 36(1):49–64.

Duffy, M. 1996. "Econometric Studies of Advertising, Advertising Restrictions, and Cigarette Demand: A Survey." *International Journal of Advertising* 15:1–23.

The Economist. 1995. "An Anti-Smoking Wheeze: Washington Needs a Sensible All-Drugs Policy, Not a "War' on Teenage Smoking." 19 August, pp. 14–15.

———. 1997. "Tobacco and Tolerance." 20 December, pp. 59–61.

Efroymson, D., D. T. Phuong, T. T. Huong, T. Tuan, N. Q. Trang, V. P. N. Thanh, and T Stone. *Decision Mapping for Tobacco Control in Vietnam: Report to the International Tobacco Initiative*. PATH Canada. Project 94-0200-01/02214.

Ensor, T. 1992 "Regulating Tobacco Consumption in Developing Countries." *Health Policy and Planning*, 7:375–81.

EPA (Environmental Protection Agency). 1992. *Respiratory Health Effects of Passive Smoking: Lung Cancer and Other Disorders*. EPA, Office of Research and Development, Office of Air and Radiation. EPA/600/6-90/006F.

Evans, W. N., and L. X. Huang. 1998. *Cigarette Taxes and Teen Smoking: New Evidence from Panels of Repeated Cross-Sections*. Working paper. Department of Economics, University of Maryland.

Evans, W. N. and M. C. Farrelly. 1998. "The Compensating Behavior of Smokers: Taxes, Tar and Nicotine." *RAND Journal of Economics* 29(3):578–95.

Evans, W. N., M. C. Farrelly, and E. Montgomery. 1996. *Do Workplace Smoking Bans Reduce Smoking?* NBER Working Paper No. 5567. Cambridge, Mass.: National Bureau of Economic Research.

FAO (Food and Agriculture Organization). 1998. Food and Agriculture Organization of the United Nations Database (http://apps.fao.org).

Federal Trade Commission. 1995. "Cigarette Advertising and Promotion in the United Sates, 1993: A Report of the Federal Trade Commission." *Tobacco Control* 4:310–13.

Foulds, J. "Strategies for Smoking Cessation." *British Medical Bulletin* 52(1):157–73.

Gajalakshmi, C. K., and R. Peto. Studies on Tobacco in Chennai, India. In Lu, R., J. Mackay, S. Niu, and R. Peto, eds. *The Growing Epidemic*, proceedings of the *Tenth World Conference on Tobacco or Health*, Beijing, 24–28 August 1997. Singapore: Springer-Verlag (in press).

Gale, F. 1997. "Tobacco Dollars and Jobs." *Tobacco Situation & Outlook*. U.S. Department of Agriculture, Economic Research Service, TBS 239(September):37–43.

———. 1998. "Economic Structure of Tobacco-Growing Regions." *Tobacco Situation & Outlook*. U.S. Department of Agriculture, Economic Research Service, TBS 241(April): 40–47.

General Accounting Office. 1989. *Teenage Smoking: Higher Excise Tax Should Significantly Reduce the Number of Smokers*. Washington D.C.

Ginsberg, S. "Tobacco Farmers Feel the Heat." *Washington Post* January 2, 1999.

Glantz, S. A., and W. W. Parmley. 1995. "Passive Smoking and Heart Disease: Mechanisms and Risk." *Journal of the American Medical Association* 73(13):1047–53.

Gong,Y. L., J. P. Koplan, W. Feng, C. H. Chen, P. Zheng, and J. R. Harris. 1995. "Cigarette Smoking in China: Prevalence, Characteristics, and Attitudes in Minhang District." *Journal of the American Association of Medicine* 274(15):1232–34.

Goto, K., and S. Watanabe. 1995. "Social Cost of Smoking for the 21st Century." *Journal of Epidemiology*, 5(3):113–15.

Gray, Mike. 1998. *Drug Crazy : How We Got Into This Mess And How We Can Get Out*. New York: Random House.

Grise, V. N. 1995. *Tobacco: Background for 1995 Farm Legislation*. Agricultural Economic Report No.709. Washington: U.S. Department of Agriculture, Economic Research Service.

Gupta, P. C. 1989. "An Assessment of Morbidity and Mortality Caused by Tobacco Usage in India." In Sanghvi, L. D. and P. Notani, eds., *Tobacco and Health: the Indian Scene*. Bombay: International Union Against Cancer and Tata Memorial Center.

———. 1996 "Survey of Sociodemographic Characteristics of Tobacco Use Among 99,598 Individuals in Bombay, India, Using Handheld Computers." *Tobacco Control* 5:114–20.

Hackshaw, A. K., M. R. Law, and N. J. Wald. 1997. "The Accumulated Evidence of Lung Cancer and Environmental Tobacco Smoke." *British Medical Journal* 315(7114):980–88.

Harris and Associates. 1989. *Prevention in America: Steps People Take—or Fail to Take—For Better Health*, cited in U.S. Department of Health and Human Services. 1989. *Reducing the Health Consequences of Smoking: 25 Years of Progress: a Report of the Surgeon General*, DHHS Publication No. (CDC) 89-8411, Office on Smoking and Health, Center for Chronic Disease Prevention and Health Promotion, Centers for Disease Control, Public Health Service, Washington, D.C.: U.S. Department of Human and Health Services.

Harris, J. E. 1987. "The 1983 Increase in the Federal Cigarette Excise Tax." In Summers L. H., ed., *Tax Policy and the Economy*. Vol. 1. Cambridge, Mass.: MIT Press.

———. 1994. *A Working Model for Predicting the Consumption and Revenue Impacts of Large Increases in the U.S. Federal Cigarette Excise Tax*. NBER Working Paper No. 4803. Cambridge, Mass.: National Bureau of Economic Research.

Hill, D. J., V. M. White, and M. M. Scollo. 1998. "Smoking Behaviours of Australian Adults in 1995: Trends and Concerns." *Medical Journal of Australia* 168 (5):209–13.

Hodgson, T. A. 1998. "The Health Care Costs of Smoking." *New England Journal of Medicine* 338(7):470.

Hodgson, T. A., and M. R. Meiners. 1982. "Cost-of-Illness Methodology: A Guide to Current Practices and Procedures." *Milbank Memorial Fund Quarterly* 60:429–62.

Hsieh, C. R., and T. W. Hu. 1997. *The Demand for Cigarettes in Taiwan: Domestic Versus Imported Cigarettes.* Discussion Paper No. 9701. Nankang (Taipei): The Institute of Economics, Academia Sinica.

Hu, T. W., H. Y. Sung, and T. E. Keeler. 1995a. "Reducing Cigarette Consumption in California: Tobacco Taxes vs. an Anti-Smoking Media Campaign." *American Journal of Public Health* 85(9):1218–22.

————. 1995b. "The State Antismoking Campaign and the Industry Response: the Effects of Advertising on Cigarette Consumption in California." *American Economic Review* 85(2):85–90.

Hu, T. W., H. Y. Sung, and T. E. Keeler, M. Marcinia, A. Keith, and R. Manning. Forthcoming. "Cigarette Consumption and Sales of Nicotine Replacement Products."

Hu, T. W., J. Bai, T. E. Keeler, P. G. Barnett, and H. Y. Sung. 1994. "The Impact of California Proposition 99, A Major Anti-Cigarette Law, on Cigarette Consumption." *Journal of Public Health Policy* 15(1):26–36.

Hu, T. W., T. E. Keeler, H. Y. Sung, and P. G. Barnett. 1995. "Impact of California Anti-Smoking Legislation on Cigarette Sales, Consumption, and Prices." *Tobacco Control* 4(suppl):S34–S38.

IEC. 1998. IEC Foreign Trade Statistics, World Bank Economic and Social Database, Washington D.C.: The World Bank.

Irvine, I. J., and W. A. Sims. 1997. "Tobacco Control Legislation and Resource Allocation Effects." *Canadian Public Policy* 23(3): 259–73.

Jenkins, C. N., P. X. Dai, D. H. Ngoc, H. V. Kinh, T. T. Hoang, S. Bales, S. Stewart, and S. J. McPhee. 1997. "Tobacco Use in Vietnam: Prevalence, Predictors, and the Role of the Transnational Tobacco Corporations." *Journal of the American Medical Association* 277(21):1726–31.

Jha, P., O. Bangoura, and K. Ranson 1998. "The Cost-Effectiveness of Forty Health Interventions in Guinea." *Health Policy and Planning* 13(3): 249–62.

Jha, P., R. Peto, A. Lopez, W. Zatonski, J. Boreham, and M. Jarvis. Forthcoming. "Tobacco-Attributable Mortality by Socioeconomic Status."

Johnston, L. D., P. M. O'Malley, and J. G. Bachman. 1998. Smoking Among American Teens Declines Some. *Monitoring the Future Study.* University of Michigan Institute for Social Research. Press release. December 18. Washington D.C.

Jones, A. M. 1999. "Adjustment Costs, Withdrawal Effects, and Cigarette Addiction." *Journal of Health Economics* 18:125–37.

Joossens, L., and M. Raw. 1995. "Smuggling and Cross-Border Shopping of Tobacco in Europe." *British Medical Journal* 310(6991):1393–97.

Jorenby, D. E., S. J. Leischow, M. A. Nides, S. I. Rennard, J. A. Johnston, A. R. Hughes, S. S. Smith, M. L. Muramoto, D. M. Daughton, K. Doan, M. C. Fiore, and T. B. Baker. "A Controlled Trial of Sustained-Release Bupropion, a Nicotine Patch, or Both for Smoking Cessation." *New England Journal of Medicine* 340(9):685–91.

Keeler, T. E., M. Marciniak, and T. W. Hu. Forthcoming. "Rational Addiction and Smoking Cessation: An Empirical Study." *Journal of Socio-Economics.*

Keeler, T. E., T. W. Hu, P. G. Barnett, and W. G. Manning. 1993. "Taxation, Regulation and Addiction: A Demand Function for Cigarettes Based on Time-Series Evidence." *Journal of Health Economics* 12(1):1–18.

Kenkel, D. S. 1991. "Health Behavior, Health Knowledge, and Schooling." *Journal of Political Economy* 99(2):287–305.

Kessler, D .A. 1995. "Nicotine Addiction in Young People." *New England Journal of Medicine* 333(3):186–89.

Laugesen, M., and C. Meads. 1991. "Tobacco Advertising Restrictions, Price, Income and Tobacco Consumption in OECD Countries, 1960-1986." *British Journal of Addiction* 86(10):1343–54.

Leu, R. E., and T. Schaub. 1983. "Does Smoking Increase Medical Expenditures?" *Social Science & Medicine* 17(23):1907–14.

Levshin, V., and V. Droggachih. 1999. "Knowledge and Education Regarding Smoking Among Moscow Teenagers." Paper presented at the workshop on "Tobacco Control in Central and Eastern Europe." Las Palmas de Gran Canaria. February 26, 1999.

Lewit, E. M., and D. Coate. 1982. "The Potential for Using Excise Taxes to Reduce Smoking." *Journal of Health Economics* 1(2):121–45.

Liu, B. Q., R. Peto, Z. M. Chen, J. Boreham, Y. P. Wu, J. Y. Li, T. C. Campbell, and J. S. Chen. 1998. "Emerging Tobacco Hazards in China. I. Retrospective Proportional Mortality Study of One Million Deaths." *British Medical Journal* 317(7170):1,411–22.

Longfield, J. 1994. *Tobacco Taxes in the European Union: How to Make Them Work for Health.* London: UICC and Health Education Authority.

Lu, R., J. Mackay, S. Niu, and R. Peto, eds. *The Growing Epidemic*, proceedings of the *Tenth World Conference on Tobacco or Health*, Beijing, 24–28 August 1997. Singapore: Springer-Verlag (in press).

Lund, K. E., A. Roenneberg, and A. Hafstad. 1995. "The Social and Demographic Diffusion of the Tobacco Epidemic in Norway." In Slama, K., ed., *Tobacco and Health.* New York: Plenum Press.

Lynch, B. S., and R. J. Bonnie, eds. *Growing Up Tobacco Free: Preventing Nicotine Addiction in Children and Youths.* Washington D.C.: National Academy Press.

Mackay, Judith, and J. Crofton. 1996. "Tobacco and the Developing World." *British Medical Bulletin* 52(1):206–21.

Mahood, G. 1995. "Canadian Tobacco Package Warning System." *Tobacco Control* 4:10–14.

Manning, W. G., E. B. Keeler, J. P. Newhouse, E. M. Sloss, and J. Wasserman. 1991. *The Costs of Poor Health Habits.* Cambridge, Mass.: Harvard University Press.

————. 1989. "The Taxes of Sin: Do Smokers and Drinkers Pay Their Way?" *Journal of the American Medical Association* 261(11):1604–09.

Maravanyika, Edward. 1998. "Tobacco Production and the Search for Alternatives for Zimbabwe." In Abedian, I., and others, eds., *The Economics of Tobacco Control.* Cape Town, South Africa: Applied Fiscal Research Centre, University of Cape Town.

Massing, Michael. 1998. *The Fix.* New York: Simon & Schuster.

McNeill, A. D., and others. 1989. "Nicotine Intake in Young Smokers: Longitudinal Study of Saliva Cotinine Concentrations." *American Journal of Public Health* 79(2):172–75.

McNicoll, I. H., and S. Boyle, 1992. "Regional Economic Impact of a Reduction of Resident Expenditure on Cigarettes: A Case Study of Glasgow." *Applied Economics* 24:291–96.

Meara, E. "Why Is Health Related to Socioeconomic Status?" Ph.D. dissertation. Department of Economics. Harvard University, forthcoming.

Merriman, David, A. Yurekli, and F. Chaloupka. "How Big Is the Worldwide Cigarette Smuggling Problem?" NBER Working Paper. Cambridge, Mass.: National Bureau of Economic Research, forthcoming.

Miller, V. P., C. Ernst, and F. Collin. 1999. "Smoking-Attributable Medical Care Cost in the USA." *Social Science & Medicine* 48:375–91.

Moore, M. J. 1996. "Death and Tobacco Taxes." *RAND Journal of Economics* 27(2):415–28.

Murray, C. J., and A. D. Lopez, eds. 1996. *The Global Burden of Disease: A Comprehensive Assessment of Mortality and Disability from Diseases, Injuries, and Risk Factors in 1990 and Projected to 2020.* Cambridge, Mass.: Harvard School of Public Health.

Musgrove, Philip. 1996. *Public and Private Roles in Health.* Discussion Paper No. 339, Washington, D.C.: The World Bank.

National Cancer Policy Board. 1998. *Taking Action to Reduce Tobacco Use.* Washington, D.C.: National Academy Press.

Niu, S. R., G. H Yang, Z. M. Chen, J. L. Wang, G. H Wang, X. Z. He, H. Schoepff, J. Boreham, H. C. Pan, and R. Peto. 1998. "Emerging Tobacco Hazards in China 2. Early Mortality Results from a Prospective Study." *British Medical Journal* 317(7170):1423–24.

Non-Smokers' Rights Association/Smoking and Health Action Foundation. 1994. *The Smuggling of Tobacco Products: Lessons from Canada.* Ottawa: NSRA/SHAF.

Obot, I. S. 1990. "The Use of Tobacco Products Among Nigerian Adults: A General Population Survey." *Drug Alcohol Dependence* 26(2):203–08.

Orphanides, A., and D. Zervos. 1995. "Rational Addiction with Learning and Regret." *Journal of Political Economy* 103(4):739–58.

Parish, S., R. Collins, R. Peto, L. Youngman , J Barton, K. Jayne, R. Clarke, P. Appleby, V. Lyon, S. Cederholm-Williams, and others. 1995. "Cigarette Smoking, Tar Yields, and Non-Fatal Myocardial Infarction:14,000 Cases and 32,000 Controls in the United Kingdom. The International Studies of Infarct Survival (ISIS) Collaborators." *British Medical Journal* 311(7003):471–77.

Pearl, R. 1938. "Tobacco Smoking and Longevity." *Science* 87:216–7.

Pekurinen, Markku. 1991. *Economic Aspects of Smoking: Is There a Case for Government Intervention in Finland?* Helsinki: Vapk-Publishing.

Peto, Richard, A. D. Lopez, and L. Boqi. "Global Tobacco Mortality: Monitoring the Growing Epidemic." In Lu R., J. Mackay, S. Niu, and R. Peto, eds., *The Growing Epidemic*. Singapore: Springer-Verlag (in press).

Peto, Richard, A. D. Lopez, J. Boreham, M. Thun, and C. Heath, Jr. .1994. *Mortality from Smoking in Developed Countries 1950–2000*. Oxford: Oxford University Press.

Peto, Richard, Z. M. Chen, and J. Boreham. 1999. "Tobacco: the Growing Epidemic." *Nature Medicine* 5 (1):15–17.

Price Waterhouse. 1992. *The Economic Impact of the Tobacco Industry on the United States Economy*. Arlington, Virginia.

Raw, Martin, A. McNeill, and R. West. 1999. "Smoking Cessation: Evidence-Based Recommendations for the Healthcare System." *British Medical Journal* 318(7177):182–85.

Reid, D. 1994. "Effect of Health Publicity on Prevalence of Smoking." *British Medical Journal* 309(6966):1441.

———. 1996. "Tobacco Control: Overview." *British Medical Bulletin* 52(1):108–20.

Reuter, P. 1992. *The Limits and Consequences of U.S. Foreign Drug Control Efforts*. RAND Cooperation Publication No. RP-135.

Rice, D. P., T. A. Hodgson, P. Sinsheimer, and others. 1986. "The Economic Costs of the Health Effects of Smoking." *Milbank Memorial Fund Quarterly* 64:489–547.

Rice, D. P., T. A. Hodgson, P. Sinsheimer, W. Browner, and A. N. Kopstein. 1986. "The Economic Costs of the Health Effects of Smoking, 1984." *Milbank Quarterly* 64(4):489–547.

Rigotti, N. A., J. R. DiFranza, Y. C. Chang, and others. 1997. "The Effect of Enforcing Tobacco-Sales Laws on Adolescents' Access to Tobacco and Smoking Behavior." *New England Journal of Medicine* 337(15):1044–51.

Roberts, M. J., and L. Samuelson. 1988. "An Empirical Analysis of Dynamic, Nonprice Competition in an Oligopolistic Industry." *RAND Journal of Economics* 19(2):200–20.

Robson, L., and E. Single.1995. *Literature Review of Studies of the Economic Costs of Substance Abuse*. Ottawa: Canadian Center on Substance Abuse.

Roemer, R. 1993. *Legislative Action to Combat the World Tobacco Epidemic*. 2nd ed. Geneva: World Health Organization.

Royal College of Physicians. 1962. *Smoking and Health. Summary and Report of the Royal College of Physicians of London on Smoking in Relation to Cancer of the Lung and Other Diseases*. New York: Pitman Publishing Co.

————. 1992. *Smoking and the Young*. London.

Rydell, C. P., and S. S. Everingham. 1994. *Controlling Cocaine: Supply Versus Demand Programs*. RAND Cooperation Publication No. MR-331-ONDCP/A/DPRC

Rydell, C. P., J. P. Caulkins, and S. S. Everingham. 1996. "Enforcement or Treatment? Modeling the Relative Efficacy of Alternatives for Controlling Cocaine." Operations Research 44(5):687–95

Saffer, Henry, and F. Chaloupka. 1999. *Tobacco Advertising: Economic Theory and International Evidence*. NBER Working Paper No. 6958. Cambridge, Mass.: National Bureau of Economic Research.

Saffer, Henry. 1995. "Alcohol Advertising and Alcohol Consumption: Econometric Studies." In Martin, S. E., ed., *The Effects of the Mass Media on the Use and Abuse of Alcohol*. Bethesda: National Institute on Alcohol Abuse and Alcoholism.

Saloojee, Yussuf. 1995. "Price and Income Elasticity of Demand for Cigarettes in South Africa." In Slama, K., ed., *Tobacco and Health*. New York, NY: Plenum Press.

Samet, J. M., D. Yach, C. Taylor, and K. Becker. 1998. Research for effective global tobacco control in the 21st century working group convened during the 10th World Conference on Tobacco or Health. *Tobacco Control*; 7(1):72–7

Schelling, T. C. 1986. "Economics and Cigarettes." *Preventive Medicine* 15(5):549–60.

Schoenbaum, M. 1997. "Do Smokers Understand the Mortality Effects of Smoking? Evidence from the Health and Retirement Survey." *American Journal of Public Health* 87(5):755–59

Scitovsky, T. 1976. *The Joyless Economy: An Inquiry into Consumer Satisfaction and Human Dissatisfaction*. Oxford: Oxford University Press.

Silagy, C., D. Mant, G. Fowler, and M. Lodge. 1994. "Meta-Analysis on Efficacy of Nicotine Replacement Therapies in Smoking Cessation." *Lancet* 343(8890):139–42.

Single, E., D. Collins, B. Easton, H. Harwood, H. Lapsley, and A. Maynard. 1996. *International Guidelines for Estimating the Costs of Substance Abuse*. Ottawa: Canadian Center on Substance Abuse.

Slama, K., ed. 1995. *Tobacco and Health*. New York, NY: Plenum Press.

Smith, Adam. 1776. *Wealth of Nations*. Edition edited by Canaan, Edwin, 1976. University of Chicago Press. Chicago.

Stavrinos, V. G. 1987. "The Effects of an Anti-Smoking Campaign on Cigarette Consumption: Empirical Evidence from Greece." *Applied Economics* 19(3):323–29.

Stigler, G., and G. S. Becker. 1977. "De Gustibus Non Est Disputandum." *American Economic Review* 67:76–90.

Stiglitz, J. 1989. "On the Economic Role of the State." In A. Heertje, ed., *The Economic Role of the State*. Cambridge, Mass.: Basil Blackwell in association with Bank Insinger de Beauford NV.

Sullum, J. 1998. *For Your Own Good: The Anti-Smoking Crusade and the Tyranny of Public Health*. New York: The Free Press.

Suranovic, S. M., R. S. Goldfarb, and T. C. Leonard. 1999. "An Economic Theory of Cigarette Addiction." *Journal of Health Economics* 18:1–29.

Sweanor, D. T., and L. R. Martial. 1994. *The Smuggling of Tobacco Products: Lessons from Canada*. Ottawa (Canada): Non-Smokers' Rights Association/Smoking and Health Action Foundation.

Tansel, A. 1993. "Cigarette Demand, Health Scares and Education in Turkey." *Applied Economics* 25(4):521–29.

Thursby, J. G., and M. C. Thursby. 1994. *Interstate Cigarette Bootlegging: Extent, Revenue Losses, and Effects of Federal Intervention*. NBER Working Paper No. 4763. Cambridge, Mass.: National Bureau of Economic Research.

Tobacco Institute. 1996. *The Tax Burden on Tobacco. Historical Compilation 1995*. Vol. 30. Washington D.C.

Townsend, Joy. 1987. "Cigarette Tax, Economic Welfare, and Social Class Patterns of Smoking." *Applied Economics* 19:355-65.

———. 1988. *Price, Tax and Smoking in Europe*. Copenhagen: World Health Organization.

———. 1993. "Policies to Halve Smoking Deaths." *Addiction* 88(1):37–46.

———. 1996. "Price and Consumption of Tobacco." *British Medical Bulletin* 52(1):132–42.

———. 1998. "The Role of Taxation Policy in Tobacco Control." In Abedian, I., and others, eds., *The Economics of Tobacco Control*. Cape Town, South Africa: Applied Fiscal Research Centre, University of Cape Town.

Townsend, Joy, P. Roderick, and J. Cooper. 1994. "Cigarette Smoking by Socioeconomic Group, Sex, and Age: Effects of Price, Income, and Health Publicity." *British Medical Journal* 309(6959):923–27.

Treyz, G. I. 1993. *Regional Economic Modeling: A Systematic Approach to Economic Forecasting and Policy Analysis*. Boston, Mass.: Kluwer Academic Publishers.

Tye, J. B., K. E. Warner, and S. A. Glantz. 1987. "Tobacco Advertising and Consumption: Evidence of a Causal Relationship." *Journal of Public Health Policy* 8:492–508.

U.S. Centers for Disease Control and Prevention. 1994. "Medical-Care Expenditures Attributable to Cigarette Smoking—United States, 1993." *Morbidity and Mortality Weekly Report* 43(26):469–72.

———. 1998. "Response to Increases in Cigarette Prices by Race/Ethnicity, Income, and Age Groups—United States, 1976-1993." *Morbidity and Mortality Weekly Report* 47(29):605–9.

U.K. Department of Health. 1998. *Smoking Kills: A White Paper on Tobacco.* London: The Stationary Office. (http://www.official-documents.co.uk/document/cm41/4177/contents.htm)

U.S. Department of Health and Human Services. 1988. *The Health Consequences of Smoking: Nicotine Addiction. A Report of the Surgeon General.* Rockville, Maryland: U.S. Department of Health and Human Services, Public Health Service, Centers for Disease Control, Center for Health Promotion and Disease Prevention, Office on Smoking and Health. DHHS Publication No.(CDC)88-8406.

———. 1989. *Reducing the Health Consequences of Smoking: 25 Years of Progress. A Report of the Surgeon General.* Rockville, Maryland: U.S. Department of Health and Human Services, Public Health Service, Centers for Disease Control, Center for Chronic Disease Prevention and Health Promotion, Office on Smoking and Health. DHHS Publication No.(CDC)89-8411.

———. 1990. *The Health Benefits of Smoking Cessation: A Report of the Surgeon General.* Rockville, Maryland: U.S. Department of Health and Human Services, Public Health Service, Centers for Disease Control, Center for Chronic Disease Prevention and Health Promotion, Office on Smoking and Health. DHHS Publication No. (CDC) 90-8416.

———. 1994. *Preventing Tobacco Use Among Young People. A Report of the Surgeon General.* Atlanta, Georgia: U.S. Department of Health and Human Services, Public Health Service, Centers for Disease Control, Center for Chronic Disease Prevention and Health Promotion, Office on Smoking and Health.

USDA (U.S. Department of Agriculture). 1998. Economic Research Service Database. (http://www.econ.ag.gov/prodsrvs/dataprod.htm)

Van der Merwe, Rowena. 1998. "Employment and Output Effects for Bangladesh Following a Decline in Tobacco Consumption." Population, Health and Nutrition Department. The World Bank.

Viscusi, W. K. 1990. "Do Smokers Underestimate Risks?" *Journal of Political Economy* 98(6):1253–69.

———. 1991. "Age Variations in Risk Perceptions and Smoking Decisions." *Review of Economics and Statistics* 73(4):577–88.

————. 1992. *Smoking: Making the Risky Decision.* New York: Oxford University Press.

————. 1995. "Cigarette Taxation and the Social Consequences of Smoking." In Poterba, J. M., ed., *Tax Policy and the Economy.* Cambridge, Mass.: MIT Press.

Wald, N. J., and A. K. Hackshaw. 1996. "Cigarette Smoking: An Epidemiological Overview." *British Medical Bulletin,* 52(1):3–11.

Warner, K. E. 1986. "Smoking and Health Implications of a Change in the Federal Cigarette Excise Tax." *Journal of the American Medical Association* 255(8):1028–32.

————. 1987. Health and Economic Implications of a Tobacco-Free Society." *Journal of the American Medical Association* 258(15):2080–6.

————. 1988. "The Tobacco Subsidy: Does it Matter?" *Journal of the National Cancer Institute* 80(2) 81–83.

————. 1989. "Effects of the Antismoking Campaign: An Update." *American Journal of Public Health* 79(2):144–51.

————. 1990. "Tobacco Taxation as Health Policy in the Third World." *American Journal of Public Health* 80(5):529–31.

————. 1997. "Cost-Effectiveness of Smoking Cessation Therapies: Interpretation of the Evidence and Implications for Coverage." *PharmacoEconomics* 11:538–49.

Warner, K. E., and G. A. Fulton. 1994. "The Economic Implications of Tobacco Product Sales in a Non-tobacco State." *Journal of the American Medical Association* 271(10):771–6.

Warner, K. E., and others. *The Medical Costs of Smoking in the United States: Estimates, Their Validity and Their Implications,* forthcoming.

Warner, K. E., F. J. Chaloupka, P. J. Cook, and others. 1995. "Criteria for Determining an Optimal Cigarette Tax: the Economist's Perspective." *Tobacco Control* 4:380–86.

Warner, K. E., G. A. Fulton, P. Nicolas, and D. R. Grimes. 1996. "Employment Implications of Declining Tobacco Product Sales for the Regional Economies of the United States." *Journal of the American Medical Association* 275(16):1241–6.

Warner, K. E., J. Slade, and D. T. Sweanor. 1997. "The Emerging Market for Long-term Nicotine Maintenance." *Journal of the American Medical Association* 278(13):1087–92.

Warner, K. E., T. A. Hodgson, and C. E. Carroll. 1999. *The Medical Costs of Smoking in the United States: Estimates, Their Validity and Implications.* Ann Arbor, MI: University of Michigan, School of Public Health. Department of Health Management and Policy. Working Paper.

Watkins, B. G. III. 1990. "The Tobacco Program: An Econometric Analysis of Its Benefits to Farmers." *American Economist* 34(1):45–53.

Weinstein, N. D. 1998. "Accuracy of Smokers' Risk Perceptions." *Annals of Behavioral Medicine* 20(2):135–40.

Wersall, J. P., and G. Eklund. 1998. "The Decline of Smoking Among Swedish Men." *International Journal of Epidemiology* 27(1):20–6.

WHO (World Health Organization). 1996a. *Investing in Health Research and Development*, Report of the Ad Hoc Committee on Health Research Relating to Future Intervention Options (Document TDR/Gen/96.1.), Geneva, Switzerland.

———.1996b. *Tobacco Alert Special Issue: the Tobacco Epidemic: a Global Public Health Emergency.* Geneva, Switzerland.

———. 1997. *Tobacco or Health: a Global Status Report.* Geneva, Switzerland.

———. 1999. *Making a Difference.* World Health Report. Geneva, Switzerland.

World Bank. 1990. *Brazil: the New Challenge of Adult Health.* Washington, D.C.

———.1992. *China: Long-term Issues and Options in the Health Transition.* Washington, D.C.

———.1993. *The World Development Report 1993: Investing in Health.* New York: Oxford University Press.

———.1994a. *Chile: the New Adult Health Policy Challenge.* Washington, D.C.

———.1994b. *Averting the Old Age Crisis.* Washington, D.C.

———.1996. *China: Issues and Options in Health Financing.* Report No. 15278-CHA, Washington, D.C.

———. 1997. *Confronting AIDS: Public Priorities in a Global Epidemic.* World Bank Policy Report. Washington, D.C.

———. 1998. *World Development Indicators.* Washington, D.C.

Zatonski, W. 1996. *Evolution of Health in Poland Since 1988.* Warsaw: Marie Skeodowska-Curie Cancer Center and Institute of Oncology, Department of Epidemiology and Cancer Prevention.

Zatonski, W., K. Przewozniak, and M. Porebski. 1999. *The Impact of Enlarged Pack Health Warnings on Smoking Behavior and Attitudes in Poland.* Paper presented at the workshop on "Tobacco Control in Central and Eastern Europe." Las Palmas de Gran Canaria. February 26, 1999.

Zhang, Ping, and C. Husten. 1998. "The Impact of the Tobacco Price Support Program on Tobacco Control in the United States." *Tobacco Control* 7(2):176–82.

Zhang, Ping, C. Husten, and G. Giovino. 1997. *The Impact of the Price Support Program on Cigarette Consumption in the United States.* Atlanta: Office on Smoking and Health, Centers for Disease Control and Prevention.

Index

DATE DUE

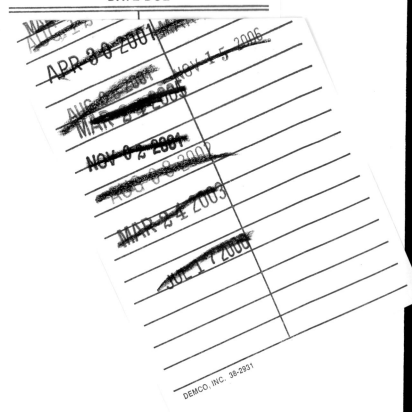